Making Sense of
Ethnomethodology

Making Sense of Ethnomethodology

Eric Livingston

Routledge & Kegan Paul
London and New York

First published in 1987 by
Routledge & Kegan Paul Ltd
11 New Fetter Lane, London EC4P 4EE

Published in the USA by
Routledge & Kegan Paul Inc.
in association with Methuen Inc.
29 West 35th Street, New York, NY 10001

Set in Imprint, 10 on 12pt
by Hope Services Ltd.
and printed in Great Britain
by R. Clay Ltd
Bungay, Suffolk

Library of Congress Cataloging in Publication Data

Livingston, Eric.
Making sense of ethnomethodology.
Bibliography: p.
Includes index.
1. Ethnomethodology.   I. Title.
HM24.L55 1987   306'.072   87–9881

British Library CIP Data also available

ISBN 0–7102–1261–5 (C)
0–7102–1262–3 (P)

For Michelle Arens
and my parents Herbert and Rosetta

Contents

Preface

I know of no academic discipline that has suffered more at the hands of its expositors than ethnomethodology. These volumes are my attempt to do better.

Making Sense of Ethnomethodology is a general introduction to ethno-methodological studies. I have, at times, sacrificed precision of expression and exactness of detail. As pedagogy, I find this preferrable to meticulous exactitude. A serious and sombre man who is drowning is a drowning man nevertheless.

The heart of any discipline sustained by discovery is its practice. As far as possible in a book, the planned sequel to this volume will teach ethno-methodological practice. It will indicate how ethnomethodology can, and in my opinion should, be taught.

Of necessity, an intellectual movement within academia places its trust in the younger generation. If these books whet the appetite of those who would learn more, they will have done their job.

Acknowledgments

Much of what is good in this book, and much of the bad that has been left out, is the result of the constant editorial assistance of Michelle Arens. After a day of work she was too often greeted with new pages of manuscript for her examination. She has saved me from numerous errors, substantive and expository, and has made this *Guide* a better book than it otherwise would have been. I benefited as well from the editorial suggestions and careful proof-reading of Rosetta Livingston; I take pleasure in acknowledging my indebtedness here. Maureen McConaghy and Charles Livingston gave valuable counsel on statistical and mathematical matters, respectively. Martin Sugarman's critical interest was a source of continual encouragement. During later stages of writing, Martin Krieger's suggestions were extremely helpful and acute. The influence of Harold Garfinkel's work is obviously reflected in these pages. In all these cases, responsibility for the text is mine alone.

In regard to copyrighted materials, I wish to thank the following individuals and publishers.

I am grateful to the literary executor of the late Sir Ronald A. Fisher, FRS, to Dr Frank Yates, FRS, and to Longman Group, London, for permission to reprint a portion of Table III from their book *Statistical Tables for Biological, Agricultural and Medical Research* (6th edition, 1974). The portion of the table I have used appears as well as part of Table D in Hubert M. Blalock Jr, *Social Statistics*, 2nd edition (New York, McGraw-Hill, 1972), itself taken from an earlier edition of the work by Fisher and Yates. I thank McGraw-Hill Book Company for their permission to use this table.

I am indebted to Macmillan Publishing Company for permission to use a portion of a transcript that appears in *Studies in Social Interaction*, edited by David Sudnow (The Free Press, a Division of Macmillan, Inc., 1972). It is reprinted by permission of the publisher. The transcript as it appears in the article 'Side Sequences' by Gail Jefferson from this book (except for the added numbering of the lines) will be found on page 67. Minor notational modifications in the transcript have been made elsewhere in the text.

I thank Cambridge University Press for allowing me to use the quote from M. S. Longair's *Theoretical Concepts in Physics* (Cambridge University

Press, 1984) that appears on page 64. The quotation is reprinted by permission of Cambridge University Press.

Throughout the writing of this book, I have benefited from the assistance and encouragement of Peter Hopkins and Terry Quigley of Routledge & Kegan Paul.

As always, my greatest debt is to my parents, my brothers, and my friends.

A guide to the reading

The chapters of this book are arranged as a pedagogic sequence. Chapters 1–5 are introductory; 6–10 illustrate some of the problems involved in studying practical action; 11–13 are an introduction to conversational analysis; 14–19 discuss an extended ethnomethodological investigation. Later chapters depend on earlier ones – for example, topics on conversation introduced in chapters 4 and 10 provide a background for the treatment of conversational analysis; the example of formatted queues is introduced first in chapter 2 and used repeatedly thereafter. More generally, the development of material in later chapters builds on and elaborates earlier discussions. Chapter 9, while discussing the statistics exercise of Chapter 8, is a self-contained introduction to ethnomethodology. It can be read independently of the statistics exercise and is central to the entire book. Chapters 14–19 on the ethnomethodology of mathematics present important aspects of ethno-methodological research, in particular because of the specificity of subject matter, illustrating both the material-specific detail involved in ethno-methodological investigations and the peculiar type of generality that arises from the consideration of such detail. I have tried to write these chapters so that the central themes will be accessible to readers unfamiliar with or uninterested in mathematics. Such readers will, perhaps, lose little by giving a cursory reading to the mathematical discussions and attending more to the discursive sections. The final chapter, 20, brings together much of the book and places the detailed consideration of conversational and mathematical materials in a larger perspective. An Index of Examples is included at the end of the text.

Chapter 1
Beginnings

In 1954[1] the Law School of the University of Chicago sponsored a study of the deliberations of trial jurors. A number of sociologists took part in the study; Harold Garfinkel was one of them. During the study, microphones were placed in a jury room, and tape recordings of the jurors' deliberations were made. For the sociologists the central question was 'How do jurors arrive at their decisions?' Associated with this question, however, was a fundamental methodological problem: What scientific, sociological methods should the investigators use in order to address the tape recordings as a faithful record of the jurors' procedures and, thereby, extract from those recordings general findings about the way juries work?

Although the details of the jury study are now part of the clouded historical past, we can imagine some of the things that must have occurred. After some issue of evidence had been debated and apparently resolved, one of the jurors might have used that evidence as part of a story intended to bring more of the trial testimony into a coherent perspective. However, when the juror came to mention the resolved issue, a different juror could have interrupted to raise the same issue once again. Several jurors sigh. After a pause in the discussion, a third juror patronizingly asks, 'Didn't we . . . didn't we already agree that the contract had to have been signed after the board of directors met?'

Had this been on the tape recordings, Garfinkel probably would have first sensed his own annoyance with the slow-witted juror who had again made problematic the resolved issue. Then he would have wondered how it was that he, too, felt that the issue had already been settled. What had the jurors done, as part of their discussion, to give the sense that some issue was, at least temporarily, resolved? How had the deliberations previously been built so as to give some utterance the appearance of it being a finalizing summary? When the same issue became problematic in the later discussion, did the jurors' sighs and the rhetorical question bring the wayward juror into line? Did the sighs serve to articulate common knowledge and, by doing so, make it that? What was the significance – if there was any – of the silence between the sighs and the next utterance? Was that hearable pause in the conversation enough to let the next speaker – the one who rhetorically asked whether or not the issue had already been settled – understand that she could take the floor from the person who had been interrupted? Was the pause between the 'didn't we's' made to establish that she was taking the floor, as well as to allow all eyes to follow her gaze to the troublemaker, therein making the intent of her question more forceful?

In such circumstances, Garfinkel must have realized, and been puzzled by the realization, that he himself understood, in a yet unarticulated manner, how the jurors were going about their work. He could hear the coherence of one juror's version of the testimony, the incoherence of another's account – the fact that something in that account didn't fit. What were the mechanisms whereby this was achieved? And what must have been equally as disturbing was that Garfinkel heard the sensibility of what the jurors were saying, not because he had been trained as a professional sociologist but because he was skilled in ordinary conversation and practiced in the ordinary activities that made up his life with others.

Listening to the tape recordings, another thing that Garfinkel must have wondered about was that, in their own way, the jurors were as concerned about what methods they should use as Garfinkel's colleagues were about their own methods. How were the jurors to weigh this bit of conflicting testimony? What issues were central to the case, and what was the proper or most efficient order in which to address them? In their own way, the jurors' concerns were just as tied to the tasks-at-hand that faced them as the sociologists' concerns were to the sociologists' tasks.

At the time of the jury study, as now, there were many legal and philosophical analyses of what constitutes truth and of how evidence should be evaluated, many psychological and social-psychological theories of how decisions are made. Something about those writings seemed wrong. From the perspective of those writings, the jurors' actual actions and reasoning provided only a distorted semblance of what, according to those writings, they should have been. Compared with what the theories indicated the jurors' actions and reasoning should have been, the jurors were deficient cogs in a theoretical machine.

Faced with this situation, Garfinkel could have introduced the distinction between 'competence' and 'performance' and assumed that the jurors knew better (competence) than they did (performance). The jurors, over the course of their deliberations, in the details of those deliberations, would then have been simply poor performers. But such a distinction only shows that theories concerning jurors' behavior are not adequate to explain the intimate details of that behavior. The proffered theories were only adequate for practical purposes – in fact, for the purposes of the academic analysts.

The discrepancy between theories of jurors' behavior and jurors' observable actions provides theorists of practical action and reasoning an endless variety of future tasks designed to bridge that discrepancy while maintaining their theoretical and research commitments. For Garfinkel, the tape recordings suggested an entirely different alternative. Undoubtably hearable on the tapes as the jurors' accomplishment, the jurors had decided the verdict.

Whatever skills they had, they were skilled in whatever was needed for them to do what they needed to do. The jurors had practical methods for accomplishing their work, and if their actions did not strictly correspond to *their own* articulated procedures, this was no different from the contrast between the actual methods of the sociologists and their espoused methodologies. In the end, then, how do people really do the things that make up the details of their lives? How do jurors reach their verdicts?

Garfinkel had come upon a huge domain of phenomena, omnipresently available, yet completely unexamined. There was no lack of writings about how decisions 'should' be made or, despite the recognized discrepancy between theory and witnessable practice, of how they 'really' are made. Yet the jurors had their own methods. Those methods were simply the methods that they used. They were not 'high falutin'' methods, but common, familiar, prosaic methods and, predominantly, the methods of ordinary conversation and natural theorizing. Similarly, the methods of the sociologists on the jury study – not the 'scientific' methods that they claimed but the ways they actually worked so that they could claim those 'scientific' methods as a faithful account of their work practices – were the recognized, familiar, 'vulgar,' unarticulated methods they used to get their work – for the practical purposes at hand – done.

In such circumstances, as a field of study rediscovering and investigating an omnipresent and ignored domain of phenomena as a domain of phenomena in its own right, ethnomethodology was born. It was to be the 'study of people's methods,' of practical action and practical reasoning.

Chapter 2
Real Settings

What is ethnomethodology?

One summer while visiting my brother, a mathematician, we met one of his friends, also a mathematician, in a record shop. As a joke, my brother introduced me as a fellow topologist. His friend was skeptical. To test me, he told me that he did not understand topology. Could I tell him what it was all about? I hemmed and hawed and then gave a textbook definition. The friend's response was that, while I was saying 'mmmm . . . mmmm . . . ahhh, topology is . . . ah . . .,' stroking my beard and looking at the floor, he had begun to believe I really was a mathematician.

Nothing is as hard, and nothing as wrong, as offering a definitive answer to the question 'What is ethnomethodology?' What ethnomethodology is is what this book is about. Yet, coupled with sufficiently detailed examples, the idea that ethnomethodology is, in some anthropological sense, the study of common, everyday methods – of practical action and practical reasoning – is enough to get started.

In this chapter, I give two examples of what I saw on my first forays into the field.

Example 1

At the beginnng of a school term the university bookstore allowed students to return books which they had purchased in anticipation of taking classes they subsequently had dropped. A row of tables had been arranged in the store and students with varying quantities of textbooks formed a single line in front of them. Three different stations had been set up where servers (student employees) would take the books and do the necessary paperwork for the returner to get a refund. The queue, the tables and the servers are schematically depicted in Fig. 2.1.

While I was watching the queue, the server on the far right became free and the second person in line helped the first carry a box of books to the open table. There were some delays in his doing this, in that it took him some time to realize that his assistance was needed.

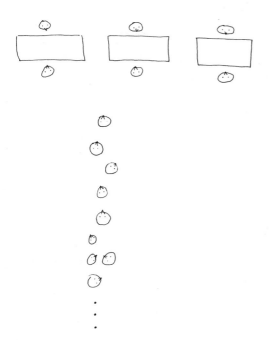

Fig. 2.1

A curious thing then happened. During the time the now first-in-line was helping carry the box of books, the server at the far left became free. People near the front of the queue began to crowd around the queue's vacant first position. Their heads were turning this way and that (Fig. 2.2). As the helper finished helping and was returning to his place at the head of the line, he saw that a server was now open, picked up the books he had left at the front of the queue (Fig. 2.2) and went to the open server. The queue then returned to a configuration resembling what it had looked like before (Fig. 2.3).

I was amazed at what I had seen. By crowding up at the front of the line and looking around, the members of the queue were witnessably inquiring as to why the proper order of the queue (which included both who was next-in-line and the length of time it should take to fill an open service bay) was not being observed. Simultaneously, they were insisting that members of the queue comply with that order. By going to his queue-determined appropriate place at the servers' tables, the queue's next-in-line eventually had complied with that queue's exhibited order. That order being demonstrated, the members of the queue repositioned themselves in a configuration similar to the original one – a configuration which again exhibited itself as a proper order of service.

5

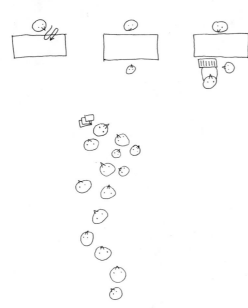

FIG. 2.2

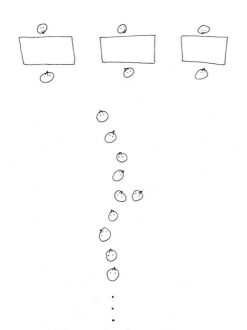

FIG. 2.3

Example 2

When I took my first classes in ethnomethodology, I was living with my parents and one of my brothers. Late in the evening my brother would sit in a rocking chair directly facing the television set; my father would sit on his left on the couch (Fig. 2.4). Every evening they would enact, and the family would witness, the same Ionescoesque drama.

FATHER It's eleven o'clock.
BROTHER [*Rocking in his chair, watching the television*] Yup.
[*Conversational silence*]
FATHER It's time for the news.
BROTHER [*Rocking*] Yup.
[*Conversational silence*]
FATHER I think we have to change channels.
BROTHER [*Still rocking*] Yup. [*Nods his head up and down*]
[*Conversational silence*]
FATHER [*Pushing himself slightly forward, starting to get up*] I'll do it.
BROTHER [*Leaning forward in the rocker, starting to get up*] No, I'll do it.
[*My father would settle back down and, almost simultaneously, so would my brother*]
FATHER [*Leaning forward, ready to push himself out of the couch*] I'll do it.
BROTHER [*Clutching the arms of the rocker and positioning the balls of his feet*] I said I'd do it.
[*My father would start, and my brother would immediately follow his lead, both resuming their normal sitting postures*]

The dance of gestures would then begin. My father would go through some emphatic motions as if he were really going to get up. My brother would respond with equally emphatic motions. Seeing my father start to relax, my brother was able to time his settling back down almost simultaneously. Pause. My father would start to get up as if he were angry, and my brother would begin to stand with equally angry compliance gestures. Both would sit down. Now Father really was angry. He would half stand. So would my brother. Both would sit down. Father actually would stand up. As soon as he started, quick as lightning, my brother would stand. Both would sit down. Occasionally they would go so far as taking first steps toward the television, then start to return to their seats, stutter-stepping in forays and retreats to the television set. I would start laughing, my brother would change channels, and Father would say, 'You're making fun of poor old dad.'

The sense that I made of this nightly spectacle was this. When my father said 'It's eleven o'clock,' he was really saying 'It's time for my son to change channels.' That is what he was saying, but he used different words. My brother knew exactly what Father had said, and he would have demonstrated that understanding by doing what had been asked of him. By saying 'Yup,' he exhibited a different understanding, namely that it was, indeed, eleven

7

F IG. 2.4

o'clock. My father, hearing what had been offered to him as what he had said, sought to repair his request by elaborating its detail – the consequentiality of it being eleven was that the news was on and, therefore, my brother should change channels. Again knowing exactly how to hear what Father was saying, my brother also understood that he could offer a different hearing that would turn the request into something else. The hearing that he offered – yes, it was time for the news – was the reason his actions did not exhibit the proper understanding of what Father had intended.

If we examine the sequence of actions when my father would 'angrily' stand up, my brother doing the same, and the two of them sitting down again, the ethnomethodological significance of this home drama becomes clearer. Both father and son were watching each other to see how the other one was doing (producing) the thing that he was doing. Even while responding by witnessably producing a next sequence of actions, both were watching the other to see what effect his responding production had on the actions that the other would do in response to it. Not only were they both using the local methods of producing an accountable social event to produce it, both were examining those witnessable methods as a means of finding what to do next.

My father was the dupe of this repeating drama, not because he was a dupe but because he wanted to watch the news and was simply trying to get his son to change channels. He was acting in a straightforward, strategic manner. My brother, on the other hand, was strategically attending to the production of the sequence of actions as a strategy. This was a vantage point once removed from my father's.

To this day my father thinks that we were making fun of 'poor old dad.' My brother had shown up his ploys for getting him to do what he wanted. Actually, what was funny was that, because of his commitment to his course of action, his 'program' – he really did not want to change the channels himself – he never saw my brother's actions as being produced to look like the things they seemed to be. Within each night's little drama, and every night once again, he was ever willing to believe that the next thing his son did was the thing that he wanted him to do.

These two examples are among the first instances where I began to see thematically, and envisage the consequentiality of seeing, organizational events and social objects – the queue, the nightly drama at home – as being locally produced, then and there, entirely with the resources their production cohort had on hand. They were examples of the local, *in situ* production of social order. Nothing in this *Guide* can replace seeing first-hand, for the first time as something of thematic interest, the production of some organizational event as the situated, local accomplishment of its production cohort in producing that event as just the event it accountably is.

Chapter 3
Naturally organized ordinary activities

In the preceding chapters an etymological definition was offered for the word 'ethnomethodology': ethnomethodology is the study of the common, everyday naturally-occurring, mundane methods that are used by people to produce and manage the common, everyday activities of the everyday social world – activities like shaking hands, taking turns-at-talk in a conversation, reaching a verdict, standing-in-line. The list could go on – proving a theorem in mathematics, asking a question, bidding in bridge, spitting and swearing, making a discovery in high-energy physics, ending a therapy session on time, diagnosing a patient's medical problem, bartering, making one's way through pedestrian traffic in rush-hour Manhattan, doing magic, performing open-heart surgery, telling gossip. Each item on the list waits for its detailed study to demonstrate its topical interest for ethnomethodological investigation.

Is ethnomethodology 'the study of people's methods?' Is it 'the study of the common, everyday methods of the common people?' For the ethnomethodologist, nothing critical depends on what definition is given to the word 'ethnomethodology'. Within the field, ethnomethodological investigations are currently referred to as studies of naturally organized ordinary activities – again, jury deliberations, shaking hands and greetings, and ordinary conversations. 'Naturally organized ordinary activities' puts emphasis on the fact that the activities under investigation are ordinary, that they are organized, and that that organization is natural in the sense that it is part and parcel of the activity itself, making that activity what it is. The activities are reflexive, self-organizing, organized entirely *in situ*, locally. That organization is not God-given, not determined by the innate properties of mind, and only obfuscated by referring to it as socialized or learned behavior – as if those terms explained what, in detail, was actually being done and, therefore, what the participants were supposed to know or to have learned.

Saying that ethnomethodology is the study of people's common, everyday methods gives an initial idea of ethnomethodology's phenomenal domain. With increased familiarity with that domain, the reader will see that the intended sense of 'commonness' is better captured by the word 'ordinary,' and that what is at question is how these ordinary activities are 'naturally organized.' What the common person knows or does not know is not at issue.

Instead, the central issue and the central research problem is the examination of the unwitting, without extrinsic motivation, production of the ordinary social object. By finding what the practically accountable social object consists of as a produced object – as the achievement of its local production cohort – the ethnomethodologist simultaneously begins to find what it means to be a member of that cohort – that is, what a member of a production cohort actually is.

In the background of their topical interests, the preceding chapters gave a glimpse of a massive domain of phenomena – the domain of practical action and practical reasoning. It is this omnipresent domain of practical methods, through which and wherein people make of the things they are doing the things that they accountably are, that the ethnomethodologist seeks to investigate. By examining those methods in the material detail of their always-idiosyncratic embodiments, the ethnomethodologist seeks to understand those methods in and as that same, endlessly diversified, identifying specificity.

Chapter 4
The problem of social order

Having introduced ethnomethodology's phenomenal domain – practical action and practical reasoning – the next task is to indicate the theoretical perspective from within which ethnomethodologists examine that domain. This is most easily accomplished with a second, apparently different, definition of ethnomethodology: ethnomethodology is the study of the production of social order.

The classic Garfinkelian example of the problem of social order is that of the 'formatted queue,' a queue like the bookstore line discussed in Chapter 2. A formatted queue's exhibited order of service, and all the order phenomena that accompany it, appear as properties of the queue that transcend its production cohort's actions. The queue appears to be completely disengaged from the work its members do to produce and maintain it. It is an immortal queue, a queue that could live forever. Yet, without the members of a queue – its local production cohort – the queue would not exist. It would have none of its local, particular-queue queue-specific properties.

In a formatted queue the queue members have come together, organized themselves, managed and monitored their actions and the actions of others so as to produce, as their achievement, this immortal yet transient object. The members of a queue position themselves, enter the queue at its exhibited end, witnessably inspect the order of the queue, distance themselves from each other, advance in observably regular ways, and orient their bodies therein to show, and showing, who is after whom, where the queue is going, where the end of the line is, who is in the queue, who is not, and who may just be visiting. In the case of the formatted queue, the order of service – and all of its associated, dependent, observable and observed properties – are produced in and as the way its production cohort has positioned itself so as to exhibit that order of service.

If an obvious example, the formatted queue is still but one example of the witnessed and produced orderlinesses of practical action. The orderliness of practical action is an omnipresent phenomenon. That orderliness resides in and makes up the everyday activities of the everyday society, whether that activity is standing in line, having a conversation, walking down a crowded corridor, proving a mathematical theorem, or producing and maintaining social distance, body orientation, directed attention and volume of speech during a conversation. The orderlinesses of practical action also make up the constraining and moral character of the social order. A person feels these constraints and this morality when she attempts to avoid standing in line by butting or by going directly to a service bay. The morality of the queue permeates the queue. It is right and proper that a particular queue, and the order-productive actions of which it consists, are the way that they are. By saying that the social order is a moral order, no judgment is being made on the intrinsic morality or immorality of practical action. The orderlinesses of practical action are simply and always interpretable; the person who butts in line is *seen* as a morally reprehensible person.

A formatted queue is, in fact, a Durkheimian social object or 'social fact.'[1] It has a transcendental presence; it appears to exist independently of the particular actions and intentions of its local production cohort; it constrains their actions; its morality pervades it; it is analyzable; its objective presence allows its interrogation; it retrospectively retains all of its properties independently of inquiries into its nature; it is seen as the source of those inquiries; and it is witnessably a produced social object. The ethno-methodological discovery and research recommendation is that the ways in which a production cohort produces and manages a particular, situated, materially-specific social object, e.g. a formatted queue, are identical with the ways in which that object – the queue – is made accountable – that it is a queue, who the first-in-line is, where the end of the line is, who is after whom. The accountability of the queue is the queue's practical objectivity; the practical analyzability of the witnessed, lived-work of the queue's production makes the queue the object that it is seen, in all its idiosyncratic particulars, to be.

By saying that ethnomethodology is the study of the production of social order and that this constraining, moral order is an omnipresent one, the ethnomethodologist also implies that there is no alternative or relief from the witnessed orderlinesses – and, therein, the practical accountability – of practical action. The analyst herself is hopelessly – irremediably – involved in the order-productive work that makes up the accountability of her research. As we shall see, the analyst is, in fact, a practical analyst of her own practical actions. On a more immediate level, however, the omnipresence of social order also means that 'social disorder' is itself an order phenomenon. It is this aspect of the 'problem of social order' that I now want to illustrate.

At one time or another we have all been in a queue where the person in front of us did not move up properly, but maintained too large a distance between herself and the person in front of her. There was something odd about the person's posture and actions that made us consider whether or not we really wanted to ask her to move up. All of our gestures and movements – our shuffling in place, impatient grimaces, our peering around her – while performing the queue-relevant task of exhibiting the queue-specific disorderly behavior of the person in front (and, therein, the queue's proper orderlinesses) are generally useless in bringing about compliance. The gestures usually take place behind the social idiot's back. They are gestures for others. If we ask her to move forward, we are often rewarded with the tiniest step in the history of humankind. Asking her to move in an authoritatively loud voice changes the request into a command; it is the attempt to give an anonymous character to the utterance, as if the queue members were speaking in unison, to bring the directed attention of others to the observable problem and thereby to shame the incompetent into conformity (see Figs 4.1 and 4.2).

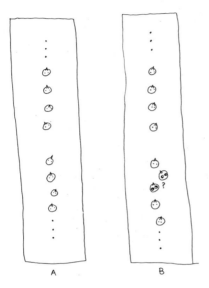

A   B

"WHAT'S   HER   GOD-DAMN   PROBLEM?"

FIG. 4.1 *'What's her goddam problem?'*

SOME #*#*! IS GOING
TO GET IN

FIG. 4.2 *'Some ***! is going to get in!'*

The apparent instance of social disorder that the maladjusted queue member produces is disorderly in that it is produced within the witnessably exhibited order of the queue. The gap in the queue is a gap because of the queue-specific distances that queue members have produced as an intrinsic feature of that queue. It is within the produced order of the specific formatted queue that the social incompetent is exhibited as being just what she is. Her witnessable incompetence is itself an order phenomenon.

A second example of the orderliness of 'social disorder' is the person who

FIG. 4.3 *'Aren't some people rude?'*

'butts' in line (Fig. 4.3). The one who butts rarely looks at the queue members behind her. In itself, this act – or non-act – is seen as the intruder's admission that she recognizes the order of service. By looking backward, not only might she encounter the queue members' angry countenances, but eye contact with the next-in-line establishes between the two of them that she is acting improperly and provides the occasion for a conversational opening without the next-in-line specifically having to work for it.

The apparent disorderliness of butting-in-line is neither random nor chaotic. It is disorderly in that it is done against the background of the witnessed orderliness of a queue as that orderliness is recognized by all the participants involved. The butt-er's errant behavior is itself a very orderly thing. We sense true evil when a person calmly walks up in front of our place in line and, without any apparent trace of emotion on her face, looks us in the eye, inviting and challenging us to make a point of her aggression. A disturbing, but order-productive phenomenon.

The ethnomethodologist studies practical action and practical reasoning as the lived-work of producing social order. Much of this *Guide* examines particular orderlinesses of the mundane society and shows how these orderlinesses and their accountable properties are locally produced, *in situ*, by their local production cohort. The preceding examples illustrate the omnipresence of that order, but things are not quite as simple as this. Central to the ethnomethodological research program is the discovery of what, in fact, the observed orderlinesses of practical action are.

To take one example, conversational turn-taking is often explained in terms of a series of rules, the first one being that 'one person speaks at a time.' The examination of actual conversations, such as the one rendered in the transcript below, shows that one speaker does not always speak at a time.[2]

ROGER I–*I* been thinkina buildin' a fallout shelter.

(1.0)

KEN hh

ROGER But I'd just throw parties th(hh)ere anywa(hh)ys hehh it'd be a fall *in*
shelte(h)r heh ⌈hh
AL   ⌊heh

KEN Hey –

(0.5)

AL heh

KEN Have you seen some a' these – fallout shelters?

ROGER Yeah, I've seen so::me,

(1.0)

ROGER Be a ⌈*nasty* place tuh hide fro(h)m
KEN   ⌊The lady –

ROGER the ⌈co(h)ps
KEN   ⌊Well – ⌈the lady up the street just-just had one put in? About
AL   ⌊hehh hh hh hhh! ha

KEN four days ago?

(DAN) Mm hm?

KEN And there's so ⌈many
ROGER   ⌊An' she threw a house war ⌈ming! hh!
KEN   ⌊Waita minute

( ) ((cough))

AL heh heh

KEN Waita minute

ROGER hh a ⌈*bomb*! hehh hh hehh hh
KEN   ⌊She's gotta *gun* in it.

KEN She's gotta gun hangin' there? And I said what's the gun for she said in
case any a' my *neigh*bors wanna come in. ⌈Yuh know?

    Later in the book I will discuss this transcribed conversational fragment in
much greater detail. For now, a cursory examination shows that often more
than one speaker speaks at a time. There are interruptions, overlaps in
speech, competition within overlaps for the next turn, organizationally
placed markers like 'Well. . .' or, in other conversations, 'Ahhh. . .' within
someone else's turn that prepare for the possession of the next one. Co-
conversationists use body movements and facial expressions to indicate that
they wish to speak next and to give definiteness to an utterance as an
uncompleted, hence anticipatory, beginning. Puzzlingly, at the same time
that this is so – that an utterance is an overlap or a next-turn marker and that
there is competition in overlaps for the next-turn – all depend on and are
practically accountable in terms of the organization of a conversation's turns
on the basis of 'one speaker at a time.'

    Analogous to queue behavior, co-conversationists are engaged in the ongoing task of formatting an order of turns. They do this within the work of turn-taking itself. Like the formatted queue, the ways in which the order of turns is exhibited – through the overlaps, the interruptions, the placed next-turn markers, the gestures and directed looks – is the production and management of that ordering of turns. Interruptions, overlaps, turn competition, turn-organization, relevant gestures exhibit and maintain the ordering of turns that they, through that exhibition and maintenance, simultaneously produce.

In this way, as at first instance, co-conversationists' work is organizational work. Co-conversationists, like the members of a queue, are engaged in the work of formatting the turns of their ongoing conversation. They format a conversation in such a way that it can be, and is, accountably done one speaker at a time (see Figs 4.4, 4.5 and 4.6). That formatting permits them to alternate turns at the appropriate pace, without reflective consideration, as the very ordinary thing that those turns and their regular alternation are produced to be. The ordinariness of a conversation's turn-taking organization, like the ordinariness of a queue's order of service, is itself a produced feature of it. Similar to a queue's exhibited order of service, the ordinariness of a

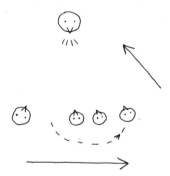

FIG. 4.4 *Formatting turns in conversation–1.*

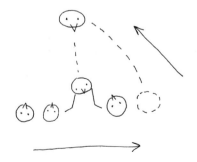

FIG. 4.5 *Formatting turns in conversation–2.*

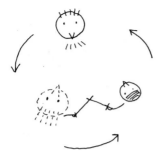

FIG. 4.6 *Two people enjoying the same formatting activity.*

conversation's turn organization is a produced ordinariness. It is produced in such a way that conversational turn organization appears to have nothing to do with the co-conversationists' actions and utterances. By co-conversationists producing a conversation in that way, the lived-work of producing the conversation has that as its exhibited, morally proper constraint – one person speaks at a time. For the ethnomethodologist, the rule 'one speaker at a time' is not *the* order of conversational turn-taking. It is the *practically accountable order* of that activity.

In retrospect, we see that we now have two apparently different definitions of ethnomethodology: one, that it is the study of practical action and reasoning; the other, that it is the study of the production of social order. The first was presented as the phenomenal domain; the second, as a theoretical perspective. The two are interchangeable. We have seen that the social order is already incorporated in practical action and reasoning ('the work which is needed to get the job done') as the unmotivated work of producing the witnessed, practically accountable orderlinesses of the social world. And we have seen that the problem of specifying the actual orderlinesses of the social world involves us in the examination of the work of their production – practical action and practical reasoning. The heart of ethnomethodology is the discovery and research recommendation that the ways in which the orderlinesses of practical action are produced and managed are identical with the ways those orderlinesses are made accountable – that they are the things that they accountably are. Ethnomethodology's fundamental phenomenon resides in the inseparability of practical action and its witnessed, produced, accountable orderlinesses.

Chapter 5

Ethnomethodological studies and problems of analysis

In the chapters that follow, the natural organization of various worldly activities will be examined. At the same time many of the chapters will illustrate problems involved in studying order-productive phenomena. Chapter 6, for example, examines how a method of analysis can produce and document a regularity of practical action that has nothing to do with the production cohort's intrinsic organization of the activity that seems to give rise to it. Chapter 8 shows how a method of analysis can give a developing structure to an array of 'data' and, from within the work of that analysis, articulate a vision of a hidden, theorized order of social action. The example of Chapter 10 illustrates how a method of analysis can specifically hide the lived orderliness of the phenomenon that the use of that method was intended to illuminate.

Although the practitioners of such methods might not describe the inadequacies of their studies in the ways an ethnomethodologist would, they themselves recognize certain prevailing deficiencies in them. The central such deficiency is the fact that, in any particular case, a documented structure or regularity of practical action is never exact. It is always, and only, adequate for the purposes at hand. Per the analyst's argument, one must understand the current situation of inquiry – including the theoretical and methodological background of the research as well as the surrounding corpus of similarly directed investigations – to understand how her research represents a further articulation of that situation of inquiry. The deficiencies of any one study make up its 'problematic' character; the aggregate of these 'problems' specifies, in part, the current context of ongoing research.

Ethnomethodologists have studied such research as a naturally organized ordinary activity in its own right. Thus, while the examples of later chapters will allow us to investigate the natural organization of various different activities, they also concern methods of analysis and research as real-worldly activities. The ethnomethodological recommendation/discovery is that, in the ways in which such research is organized so as to produce practically adequate findings, the 'problems' illustrated in the next few chapters inhabit such research in an irremediable way. Practitioners recognize the deficiencies of their studies; they continually seek to repair them. The 'problems' provide the origins and motives for future studies. Yet, in the ways in which those reparative procedures are again part of an ongoing, naturally organized activity organized to produce practically accountable findings, every attempt to repair them reincorporates the same identifying features of the activity that give rise to and produce the 'problems.'

Practitioners' recognition of the practical character and practical adequacy of their studies serves to identify a class of studies of practical action and reasoning. In the ways in which they are conducted, these studies irremediably hide the order-productive phenomenon of practical action and reasoning, both in the intended objects of the research and in and as their own methods. This itself being a technical order-productive phenomenon, the name 'classical studies of practical action' has been given to such research. The term is not used to define or encompass a phenomenon, but suggestively to name a discovered phenomenon in terms of its discovered properties. The further examination and illumination of such phenomenon is the aim of ethnomethodological research, not the establishment of proper classificatory definitions.

So far, then, there are at least four ways to view the examples of the next chapters: as illustrations of order-productive phenomena; as exhibiting the essential and irremediable ties between analytic methods and the naturally organized ordinary activities in which they occur and, therein, such methods as order production phenomena; and as instances of two ethnomethodological discoveries – first, that one's methods can irremediably hide those methods' own order-productive work and, second, the existence of classical studies. The situation is further complicated by a number of other ethnomethodological perspectives that can be brought to bear on the activities that the examples report. To name two, there is the research problem of what makes up the identifying detail of a social object for it accountably to be that object for its local production cohort, and the problem of investigating the relationship between description and argumentation.

At some point, usually when someone actually takes part in an ethnomethodological investigation, this complexity cannot be avoided. In fact an ethnomethodologist worries when that complexity (or phenomenal richness and depth) is not present. For now, it is better to view the examples somewhat naively. In the end, the phenomenal presence of activities such as those described in the following chapters is the touchstone of all ethnomethodological theorizing.

Chapter 6
Pedestrian traffic flow

A number of years ago, in the days before the videotape gold rush, a sociologist in New York became interested in studying pedestrian traffic flow. As a means of doing so, he positioned a camera on the roof of a building and made films of people crossing a signal-monitored intersection in Manhattan. The films showed numerous examples of two streams of pedestrians, first massing on opposing corners, then managing to interpenetrate each other and permit their mutual passage. The films indicated that such passage is made in an endless variety of ways; hence, that it cannot be explained by citing a simple rule. A rule like 'passage is made on the right' is obviously incorrect. The diverse and changing character of the traffic flow was itself a feature of the pedestrians' interaction for which an explanation was sought. The sociologist's argument, which he documented in the films through the use of still frames and stop action sequences, was that pedestrians form themselves into 'wedges' and 'fronts' behind 'point people.' This structure of bodies, so the argument went, allowed pedestrians to navigate through each other. When the films were reshown at film speed and interpreted in these geometric terms, the pedestrians' diverse movements appeared to be in these describable – and hence coherent – patterns (see Fig. 6.1).

FIG. 6.1 *As seen by General Haig from his helicopter.*

The problem posed by these films is an interesting one, an example of what is termed 'collective behavior.' The name refers to the fact that a sizable production cohort brings about concerted action (like directional stampeding) while its members maintain their absolute anonymity to each other, as members of that cohort, throughout the activity's entire production and accomplishment. In the case of the pedestrian traffic flow, the particular problem posed by the films was that an observably large number of people were amassed on opposing corners of the intersection. Within seconds, they organized themselves, while preserving their anonymity, in such a way that they could pass each other in an efficient manner, with minimal body contact, in the time that the motorists and traffic signal allowed. How did they do this? Those of us who have visited New York and found ourselves for the first time in the front wave of a rush hour street crossing know the trepidation of entering into the action. Having completed the crossing, its accomplishment seemed amazing and somewhat mysterious. The question that the film demonstration raised was whether or not pedestrians actually use 'wedges,' 'fronts,' and 'point people' – the structures documented in the films – to get the job done.

The perspective of 'wedges,' 'fronts' and 'point people' is, of course, from a vantage point that none of the participants had or could have. Pedestrians do not use these documented, geometrically described alignments of physical bodies; they are engaged in a much more dynamic forging of their paths. They are engaged in locally building, together, the developing organization of their mutual passage. That organization is, and accommodates itself to, the witnessable structures of accountable action as they develop over the course of their journey.

To understand how pedestrians manage their crossing we must, metaphorically, move the camera to eye level. When a pedestrian goes 'out of the gate' quickly, her attention is focused on the others crossing the intersection in the opposite direction. As the movement of the opposing army and its leaders becomes clear, she adjusts her path. In fact, she can begin to do this before the actual crossing is under way. She inspects the alignment of pedestrians on the opposite corner and sees those who, like herself, have eagerly positioned themselves to be 'front runners.'

Even before a 'front runner' or 'scout' comes into physical proximity with the opposing flow, the small group of people in front of her observable path begin to move so as to allow a place for her passage. The people behind the bifurcating interface see this directed movement and begin to orient themselves toward following those in front, continuing their motion in that direction. While this is going on, the 'scout' has already headed for, and moved into, the opening that is being provided for her.

Like the 'scout,' while beginning to come together the members of the two opposing sides similarly move while watching the others to see how they are moving, both toward apparent places of passage and to allow the passage of the opposing stream. In particular, they attend to the developing paths of the 'front runners.' They move in behind those trajectories, looking for the places that the 'scouts' are both finding and helping to produce. Seeing the place of passage that the 'scout' is moving toward and into, the others behind her see that place as a place of passage and angle toward it. The members of the 'first wave' adjust their paces to permit this directional movement.

From within this organizational activity as it develops, the opposing flow of pedestrians appears as a moving, somewhat plastic wall. The directional movement, proximity, closeness of steps, and body orientations of its constituents do not provide seeable gaps for counter-directional movement other than those that the movement as a whole is heading toward and into. During the initial organization and throughout the continuing passage, this lack of alternative gaps is produced, in part, so as not to allow counter-directional movement and, in part, under the pressure of maintaining an appropriate distance from the swelling horde behind. Those not in the 'first wave' become trapped by this mass of directed movement and follow in its wake. They immediately fill the single-step places that the movement ahead and at their sides permits and that the movement of the entire surrounding army demands they fill with the appropriate, cohort-determined pace (Fig. 6.2).

During the ongoing course of the crossing, the pedestrians are intrinsically building the interface between their two conflicting currents. That interface as it is seen and produced by the pedestrians is quite different from the way it appeared on the sociologist's films. When it is seen on films made from above, the interface itself provides the films' witnessable phenomenon. Through his interest in accounting for pedestrians' behavior in terms of documented, regular, repeating structures of practical action, the sociologist attempted to render that interface through the use of geometric figures. The phenomenal basis of his theorizing – the pedestrians' production and maintenance of an interface between the two oppositely directed currents of walkers – was hidden by his methods of analysis and his natural theorizing.

This contrasting description of pedestrians' organizational work is a first guide to the action; it is not a detailed ethnomethodological analysis. It gives an idea – or, as an ethnomethodologist would say, technical access to – the intrinsic, locally produced, *in situ* organization of the walk across the crowded intersection. The preferred usage – 'technical access' – emphasizes that a description or account is not a disengaged, objective finding although it can be presented as such. The description allows someone to visit such crowded intersections and elaborate the description in terms of the actual lived-details of the organizational work of pedestrian street crossings. The description is itself a pedagogy that has real-world street crossings as its referent. Its claim to adequacy is that, by using it, one can get access to the technical details of how pedestrians themselves manage their passage through each other.

One feature of the foregoing description, however, does deserve further consideration. The successful passage of the two pedestrian armies critically

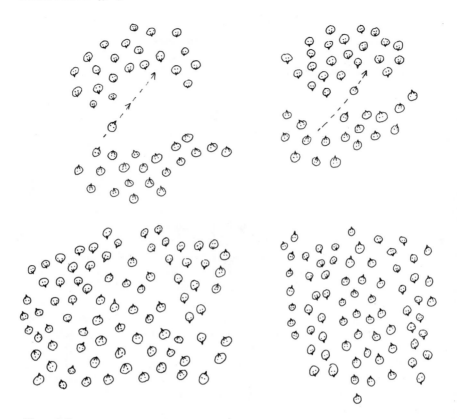

F<small>IG</small>. 6.2

depends on the varied paces of the members of their respective 'first waves.'
It would be easy to say that this feature of the crossing is insured by a random
distribution of walking paces in the pedestrian population or that, probabilis-
tically, some individual is always going to be in a hurry. This is simply, and
interestingly, not so.

A person in a hurry knows that she must be the first one 'out' in order not
to be trapped by the pace internally generated after the organization of the
passage has begun to be developed. These 'rushers' are seen by both fronts;
they take eager, anticipatory steps before the intersection has cleared; their
purposefulness is a witnessed feature of their comportment and demeanor;
because of this, they are sometimes saved by others from serious vehicular
injury. More generally, however, independent of any extrinsic motivation
that can be attributed to individual members of the production cohort, the
varied paces of the members of the 'first wave' are themselves an
organizational phenomenon. As the two pedestrian flows begin to come into
proximity with each other, the developing organization of the horde
encroaching from behind and at their sides, and the movements and

beginning bifurcation of the interface ahead, constrain the members of the 'first wave' to quicken or slow their pace so as to find and fill the openings of passage that are being made available to them and that they, reciprocally, are making available to the opposition. The first ones 'out of the gate' – the 'scouts,' 'rushers,' 'front runners,' or 'interference people' – are, in fact, working in concert with all parties. They do what is practically necessary to get the crossing organized in the way that the developing structure of that crossing demands that it be done. The interesting thing about their actions is that those actions are themselves constrained features of the developing, lived-orderliness of the produced passage and crossing.

Against this background, the geometric description of the pedestrians' movements in terms of 'wedges,' 'fronts,' and 'point people' is at best a documented residue of the naturally organized lived-work of getting through traffic. It is not the intrinsic structure of that work. The practical actions involved in crossing the intersection are simply not orchestrated in that manner. The participants are engaged in the ongoing, *in situ* organization of the passage, and they themselves are producing, managing, and accomplishing its accountable features as those features are available to the participants themselves. In fact, 'orchestrated' is the wrong word entirely. It surreptitiously reintroduces the existence of the disengaged observer placed above the action like the camera. It is a vantage point that none of the production cohort have, and it suggests that the actions of that cohort are obeying some external, mundane force. The geometric descriptions offered from such a position are, at best, only an approximate – or, given the naturally organized activity in which that description is a part, a practically adequate – external description of the structure of the pedestrians' actions *even as they are available on the films*.

Generally speaking, the analyst recognizes that the descriptions she offers are not really precise. This is not because an alternative description/analysis is available, but because the descriptions she provides do not quite fit what is observable on the streets, in the experimental setting or, in this case, on the films. She recognizes that there is a discrepancy between her theorized descriptions and the actions of the production cohort. Despite the fact that the pedestrians *could* be seen to be joining 'wedges' and 'fronts' and building them together, the chains of bodies only approximated the geometric figures. The pedestrians formed 'sort of' wedges and 'sort of' curvilinear fronts. The movements of some individuals did not conform to the envisioned lines of action. Various troops branched off or became isolated pools of movement. In addition, the films, and the demonstration sequences of sequential still frames that were extracted from those films, raised questions that they themselves could not be used to answer. What, for example, were the variety of individual body orientations and directed eye movements? Are these irrelevant to the claimed structure of the pedestrians' concerted actions? How do the altered paces of the walkers and the shifting 'angles,' the 'protuberances,' and the 'gaps' in the interface tie in with the claimed geometric structures?

Recognizing these imprecisions – and, hence, the discrepancy between her descriptions and observed behavior – the analyst tries to repair them. On one hand, she seeks to refine her demonstrations; on the other, she seeks to account for deviant actions and bring them into a more finely textured, wider ranging perspective. One alternative is to break the production cohort's actions into 'building blocks' or 'structural units' similar to the familiar representation of molecules swimming in some fluid, looking for and bonding with others to form larger molecular structures (Fig. 6.3). These more basic structures are used to provide an explanation for the pedestrians' actions that previously did not conform to the hypothesized patterns. The pedestrians are interpreted as strategically using these more basic, 'phenomenal' units to build the structure of their movements as that structure is available to the heavenly positioned observer. The films are re-examined and re-analyzed, and new sequences of still frames are extracted to document this more fundamental organization. Curiously, when the analyst addresses the problem of how the production cohort actually produces and manages the intersection crossing, she understands by this one of three things: that her original description is such an explanation; that the description is such an explanation when coupled with an elected, appropriate theory of practical action (behaviorist, genetic, social learning, or otherwise); or that what is needed is a theorized construct like 'structural units' that accounts for the

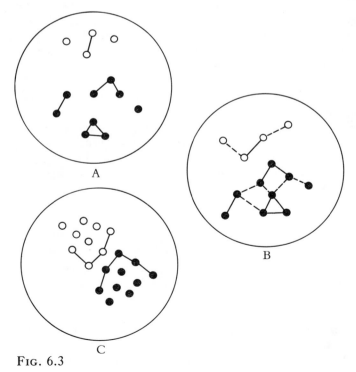

Fig. 6.3

original, hypothesized, geometric structures and the apparent deviations from them.

The sociologist's original films were artfully made and used so as to produce the purported demonstration of the existence of geometrically described regularities of the pedestrians' actions. The position of the camera, the distance at which the films were made, and the width of the camera's field allowed one to see the general aggregate movement. They did not permit an examination of the pedestrians' directional orientations, facial work, and the minutiae of their bodily adjustments to the closing proximity of the others. That the pedestrians formed 'wedges' and linear 'fronts' (and, therein, that the 'scouts,' 'front runners,' or 'interference people' were to be seen as *'point* people') was a feature of the crossing *only* witnessable from that perspective. Still frames and stop action were used to document the existence of these structures. Yet, in the succession of stopped frames, the progressive distances of the approximate 'fronts' were not evenly paced. The lateral shifts of the geometric figures seen through the series of stills remained unaccounted for. In fact, as the reader will recall, the films shown at film speed originally posed the problem of explaining the witnessed diversity of the pedestrians' movements. In brief, the purposefulness of the construction of the demonstration footage was to invite its observers to *interpret* what pedestrians witnessably do in the terms that the demonstration sought to provide, even though 'what pedestrians witnessably do' remained, and was recognized as remaining, problematic throughout.

The reader may feel that the problems we have encountered are not *per se* the result of the methodology that the sociologist employed. Rather, the difficulties were caused either by the methodology's inappropriate use or the researcher's individual lack of perspicuity. This is not the case. The problems arise even though, and because, the methodology is a professionally acceptable or adequate – or good – one. The analyst will readily agree that something might be wrong with her method of examining the particular phenomenon in question. That something is essentially wrong with her methods or that her methods are simply instances of the same phenomenal domain is, for her, an impossible suggestion. For the analyst, a proof of this would require the use of other methods to demonstrate what the 'real' disengaged structure of the activity is. In order for the demonstration to be acceptable, the methods used to produce it would have to be similar, in yet unspecified ways, to hers. Her familiarity with the practically adequate, order-productive thing that her own methods are and must be tells her that such a demonstration is impossible. So it is. Given her professionally accountable ways of working, the same problems will continually arise.

In the case of pedestrian traffic flow, we have seen that the reliance on appropriate methods of analysis and documentation can hide the order-productive character of pedestrians' practical actions and reasoning. To see that this is essentially so, we must first examine the type of naturally organized ordinary activity such an analysis is.

Chapter 7
Local practice and freeway traffic

This chapter develops an example that is due to Garfinkel. The discussion of it summarizes much of the text to this point while introducing a number of issues that will gain in importance as this *Guide* progresses.

Sometimes on the freeway, drivers will be forced to slow down and stop. They will search the terrain for the cause of the change in the previous, locally stabilized pace of traffic. Realizing that there are widening gaps between their cars and the cars ahead, and that the cars around them have begun to accelerate, they respond by accelerating as well. Continuing their search for the cause of the disturbance, seeing a stalled car on the side of the road, they see this as the reason for the previous slowdown.

Various aspects of order-productive phenomena are illustrated through this regularly occurring circumstance. First, as a driver begins to slow in response to the surrounding traffic, she begins a situated inquiry. She looks around to see 'what's holding up traffic?' Garfinkel's answer was 'you are.' His point was that the drivers' own actions, among which were their inquiry and scanning for 'what's holding up traffic,' created and preserved the situation in which they had to slow and stop their cars. The drivers' own practices as competent drivers in a local cohort producing their own immediate driving conditions – whether maintaining a locally stabilized driving pace and inter-vehicular distance or responsively slowing to the stoppage ahead – provided the local origins and motives for the inquiry. That inquiry and its appropriateness were themselves features of the cohort's order-productive work.

This example illustrates how an inquiry is an occasioned, situated feature of the activity in which and of which it is a part. The previously witnessed, produced, and managed local stability of driving speed and the following stoppage occasioned the inquiry into the causes of the traffic disturbance. Ironically, it is that inquiry that preserves the disturbance and, in that way, provides its own organizational-specific origins.

At the same time, this example also illustrates that an account – the 'reason' for the disturbance in the traffic flow – is a feature of the ongoing, developing activity as well. If the drivers see crumpled vehicles on the side of the road, they see in their probable history the original cause of the problem. Noticing that the drivers in front of them have turned to stare at the scene, they blame bad driving habits. If, after driving farther, traffic again begins to slow, they think 'the real trouble is still ahead.' Finding a stalled car in the middle of traffic, they may attribute the blocked flow to that or to the fact that some drivers are too scared or incompetent to look for and move into open lanes and that others are not providing them with regularly paced places to move into. The succession of stops and relatively stable movement during rush hour are seen simply as 'traffic as usual,' the conditions of rush-hour traffic flow. Similarly, the account that a driver is 'staring,' 'scared,' or 'incompetent,' that someone is a 'speedster' or has 'missed her turn-off,' that traffic has provided an 'opening' or an 'opening she could have moved into' – and the practical adequacy of such accounts – are produced features, and illustrations of, the cohort's order-productive work. Unavoidably, practical reasoning fills the world and makes up its observed and reportable events.

The drivers' own accounts of the stalled traffic and the practical adequacy of those accounts, like the original inquiry, are essentially tied to the developing circumstances of their driving with and among others. Whether or not their inquiry has an extra-organizational referent – the stalled car – or an inter-organizational one – the drivers' examination of their own driving practices or 'traffic as usual' – is a driver's practical achievement. It is essentially and irremediably tied to her order-productive work as a member of the local cohort of drivers producing together their immediate driving circumstances. Whether or not a stalled car is seen as the cause of the disturbance is itself a feature of the ongoing activity. The practical adequacy of that account resides in the way in which the account is tied to the activity of which it is a part as well. There is no disengaged objective situation, only the practically objective circumstances as they are produced and witnessed by the production cohort and formulated in the description 'there's a stalled car over there.'

In part, ethnomethodological research is directed toward examining the detailed ways in which accounts are essentially tied to the activities of which they are a part. The adequacy of ethnomethodological studies depends on the way they provide technical access to that intrinsic dependency.

There is still another lesson that this example offers. Drivers are themselves lay analysts of practical action and practical reasoning. This is shown in their inquiry into 'what's holding up traffic?' But, moreover, as lay analysts, they produce and maintain the driving cohort's local driving conditions. They scan traffic to find accountable gaps in order to change lanes. They monitor their relative speed and their speedometers, and regulate pressure on the gas pedal, in order to maintain the cohort's locally stabilized speed and inter-vehicular distance. In traffic jams they use occasioned devices like distinguishable vehicles to time the relative pace of cars in other lanes. Seeing the congestion on an on-ramp, drivers will force their way into the center lanes which, in turn, distributes and exacerbates the problem. That they 'force' their way into another lane is itself the practically adequate account of their actions and is essentially tied to the witnessable gaps and the witnessed pace of those gaps in the surrounding traffic. The poor driver, herself an order-production phenomenon, is exhibited from within this background. So is the driver who has 'just missed her turn-off.' And the speedster uses and depends on this witnessed, local production of the immediate conditions of traffic flow to weave her way into the local anomaly.

Drivers, as well as professional analysts – systems engineers in the case of traffic flow – are, hopelessly, practical analysts of practical action. As such, they produce and manage the ordinary orderlinesses of their unavoidable, hopelessly practical, practical activities. Their inquiries, accounts, descriptions, and analyses are all part of their ongoing activities and gain their practical adequacy as part of those developing activities as well.

Drivers, as members of a production cohort – and as members of a production cohort, as analysts of its and their own order-productive work – produce and maintain the witnessable details of their local driving circumstances. The ways that they do so are identical with the ways that they make their driving 'account-able' – they are witnessably changing lanes, slowing down, trying to get to the off-ramp. Therein, they produce together the relatively stable features of freeway traffic flow. These consist, in fact, of their relatively stable, locally produced and regulated driving practices.

Taking this one step further, we see that the successes of professional analysts – such as they are – critically depend on just this stability. The systems engineer will build a mathematical model of the traffic flow. She will measure traffic density, average speed, number of lanes, and the physical arrangement of interchanges and on- and off-ramps. Comparing that model to models of other real or imagined freeway constructions, she will make her recommendations. Incorporated into a freeway's design, those recommendations will have a practically accountable impact on traffic flow. But that impact will result because of the relative stability of the cohort's driving practices. That relative stability of practice allows the systems engineer to modify her models and examine the possible consequences. If tomorrow those driving practices were to change radically – if, for example, drivers controlled their speeds in strictly graded and self-monitored lanes and began 'naturally' (as a feature of the ongoing, natural organization of driving practice) to produce greater inter-vehicular distances or, on the other hand, if they did the exact opposite – entire patterns of traffic flow would change.

Thus, there is at least one more lesson to be gained from this example. While professional analysts use and rely on drivers' local driving practices, those practices enter into their models, architects' designs, and actual constructions in a surreptitious manner. They are things that the architect and construction engineer know have to be incorporated into the construction; they are essential, unthematicized relevancies of traffic flow. Although a freeway's design-analysis will have its impact on those practices, the analysis itself is completely uninstructive – except in inadvertent ways – in the details of what the drivers are doing to provide the stable conditions that permit the analysis. The traffic flow production cohort's practices and the order-productive character of those practices – the phenomena of practical action and reasoning – are the ghosts in the machine that make it work.

Chapter 8
A statistics exercise

The following is a slightly modified version of an exercise given to students in an introductory class on the statistical methods of sociology. It was assigned early in the course, prior to the lectures on sampling and hypothesis testing, and was intended to help teach sociologists' mathematical methods as *praxis*. I have included the numerical solutions and a variety of 'answers' to the non-numerical questions. The discussion of the last question gives the exercise an ethnomethodological twist.

The exercise

As part of a study of academic workload, a random sample was taken of sociologists at fifteen top-ranked sociology departments in the United States. All of the professors in the population from which the sample was drawn had received tenure between 1961 and 1980. An index was constructed to measure a faculty member's number of professional publications. Each entry in the array in Table 8.1 represents the total number of publications a distinct faculty member had in the year of tenure and the five years preceding it.[1]

Table 8.1 Number of publications of each professor

2	2	3	9	6	9	7	9	6	3
3	10	8	5	10	4	9	6	4	4
9	7	7	11	8	9	5	5	8	6
9	10	5	6	6	7	5	8	10	7
7	6	4	2	8	10	5	3	10	8
4	11	9	9	6	10	7	6	10	8
10	7	7	5	4	11	8	8	6	11
3	12	4	9	7	2	12	5	7	5
9	8	1	3	13	4	8	6	9	6

QUESTION 1

Make a frequency table for the sample, compute the mean, and draw a frequency polygon.

Solution

Table 8.2 Frequency table for the total sample

Number of publications	Frequency	(Frequency) × (Number of publications)
0	0	0
1	1	1
2	4	8
3	6	18
4	8	32
5	9	45
6	12	72
7	11	77
8	11	88
9	12	108
10	9	90
11	4	44
12	2	24
13	1	13
	$N = 90$	Sum = 620

The frequency table is shown in Table 8.2. From this table:

Mean = Average number of publications per faculty member
= Sum/N
= 6.9

Fig. 8.1 shows the frequency polygon.

After the sample was taken someone suggested that there might be a difference in the distribution of numbers of publications between the relatively older and the relatively younger faculty members. The sample was divided into two groups: Array I (Table 8.3) is for those faculty members tenured between 1961 and 1970; Array II (Table 8.4) is for those tenured between 1971 and 1980.[2]

Table 8.3 Array I, for those tenured between 1961–70

2	3	4	5	6	7	8	9	10	11
2	3	3	10	9	8	7	6	5	4
4	3	5	4	6	5	7	9	8	5
6	7	8	4	5	6	7	4	8	5
6	7	8	5	6	7	8	6	6	6

Table 8.4 Array II, for those tenured between 1971–80

1	2	3	4	5	6	7	10	8	9
11	12	13	9	8	7	6	5	4	3
10	11	12	7	8	9	10	11	10	10
10	10	7	8	9	9	9	9	9	9

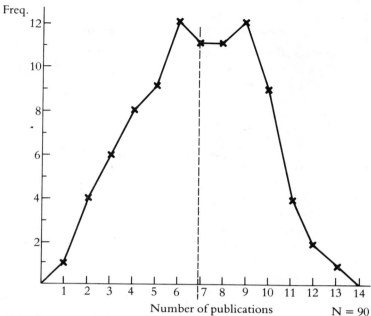

Fig. 8.1 *Frequency polygon (total sample).*

QUESTION 2

Make frequency tables for each of the subsamples, but this time include
columns for the percentage of the subsample in each category and the
cumulative percent. Why can't you use the frequencies to compare the two
groups directly?

Solution

Table 8.5 *Frequency table Array I*

Number of publications	Frequency	(Frequency) × (Number of publications)	Percent	Cumulative percent
1	0	0	0	0
2	3	6	6	6
3	4	12	8	14
4	6	24	12	26
5	7	35	14	40
6	10	60	20	60
7	7	49	14	74
8	7	56	14	88
9	3	27	6	94
10	2	20	4	98
11	1	11	2	100
	$N = 50$	Sum = 300		

33

Table 8.5 shows the frequency table for Array I. From this table:

$\bar{x}_I$ = Mean of I = Sum/N = 6
Mo_I = Mode of I = Category with highest frequency[3] = 6
Mdn_I = Median of I = the number of publications for which an equal
          number of professors had less and more[3]
        = 6

Table 8.6 shows the frequency table for Array II. Again, from this table:

Table 8.6 Frequency table for Array II

Number of publications	Frequency	(Frequency) × (Number of publications)	Percent	Cumulative percent
1	1	1	2.5	2.5
2	1	2	2.5	5.0
3	2	6	5.0	10.0
4	2	8	5.0	15.0
5	2	10	5.0	20.0
6	2	12	5.0	25.0
7	4	28	10.0	35.0
8	4	32	10.0	45.0
9	9	81	22.5	67.5
10	7	70	17.5	85.0
11	3	33	7.5	92.5
12	2	24	5.0	97.5
13	1	13	2.5	100.0
	$N = 40$	Sum = 320		

$\bar{x}_{II} = 8$
$Mo_{II} = 9$
$Mdn_{II} = 9$

It does not make sense to compare frequencies between the two subsamples because the sample sizes are different. If, in a sample of 100 professors, ten had published six papers, and if, in another sample of ten professors, 'only' one had published six papers, the same percentage of faculty members in both samples would have published six papers. That a smaller number had published six papers may be a result of the sizes of the samples, not an intrinsic difference between them. In some way we must normalize the two samples so we can compare them. This is what we are doing by computing the percentages in each category. In hypothesis testing, different methods will be used.

QUESTION 3

Draw frequency polygons for these two distributions using the number of publications as the abscissa and the percent of faculty as the ordinate.

Distinguish the two by using a solid line for Array I and a dotted line for Array II, and label them accordingly. Mark the means, medians, and modes on the abscissa.

Solution

See Fig. 8.2.

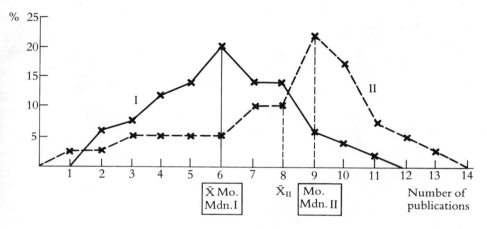

FIG. 8.2 *Percentage polygons for subsamples.*

QUESTION 4

Compare the two polygons (distributions) in terms of their general shape and location. Summarize what this means in terms of the number of publications and the two groups of faculty. Compare the two subsamples to the original, total sample using the graphs. Does there seem to be some relationship emerging between the subsamples that 'needs' to be explained?

Answers

Students generally know only one curve to compare with the polygons, the Gaussian distribution or normal curve. It is often described as having a bell shape and looks something like the Fig. 8.3. In the Gaussian distribution the mean, median, and mode coincide.

FIG. 8.3 *Gaussian or normal distribution curve.*

35

All of the polygons in Figs 8.1 and 8.2 more or less approximate to this distribution. The polygons for the original sample (Fig. 8.1) and subsample I (in Fig. 8.2) approximate to a symmetric distribution; the polygon for subsample II in Fig. 8.2 is skewed to the left. (Skewed left means that the bulk of the distribution – actually, most of the area under the polygon – falls into the right part of the distribution, the side with higher numbers of publications.) The mean of subsample I is less than the mean of subsample II. On the average the professors (in the sample) tenured in the 1970s were publishing more prior to tenure than those tenured in the 1960s. The symmetric character of the polygon for the total sample (Fig. 8.1) seems to mask the fact that a change has occurred. The 'older' professors published less and the number of their individual publications seems to have been more uniform. The 'new' faculty is publishing more but less uniformly, with an increasing number of faculties publishing more.

The shift in means may suggest that tenure standards are becoming more stringent or that faculty are seeing publication rate as a means of insuring tenure. The fact that the polygon for subsample II is skewed left may indicate that the 'younger' faculty are responding to increased competition, to increasing uncertainty concerning tenure, are more aggressive academicians than their predecessors, or that publication rate is an avenue to professional recognition, providing access to dwindling funds and resources.

A novel answer is that the difference in means indicates the rapidity with which the science of sociology is progressing, the skewness pointing to the fact that the younger faculty tend to be on the forefront of knowledge, only a few of them simply exploiting their graduate background.

The problem that arises is that of explaining the apparent differences between the publication rates of the two subsamples.

QUESTION 5

Think of names for subsamples I and II and explain your reasons for those choices. Label your tables and graphs accordingly.

Answers

Given that the two subsamples seem to reflect a change in the population, names indicating this seem appropriate.

'Old order'/'new order' suggests there has been a change in social structure. 'Old regime'/'new regime' indicates that the change reflects imposed constraints. 'Old hands'/'new practitioners' points to a difference in work practices. 'Scholars'/'professionals' seems pejorative, but it may be the general perspective that a student is trying to articulate through the exercise. 'Good times'/'bad times' or 'good times'/'hard times' emphasizes economic factors or, more generally, the larger educational and societal context in which academic sociologists work. 'Old timers'/'new timers' seems a bit dull, but it trades on the understanding that those tenured later most likely would be younger faculty.

The reason for labeling the tables and graphs is that, with those titles attached, the tables and graphs are seen as illustrating something about the distinction that the titles make available. For example, the labels 'old regime'/'new regime' point to the fact that something not yet analyzed is prospectively different about the two 'regimes.'

QUESTION 6

Give an explanation for the faculty whose scores (number of publications) fall in the left tail (the extreme left) of polygon II in Fig. 8.2.

Answers

Those on the extreme left were faculty whose tenure apparently was not influenced by their lack of publications. Early tenure, and the fact that those professors were previously students, is a possible explanation, but it suggests another cause.

These faculty members were seen by their colleagues to be extremely bright. Their few publications reflected that brilliance, and their unpublished work merited the tenure decision. Alternatively, their tenure could reflect extra-departmental politics and university hiring practices. Or these faculty members might perform services for the department like obtaining large grants. They could also be seen as political hustlers.

QUESTION 7

Approximate the area shared under graphs I and II in Fig. 8.2 and the total area under both. If the graphs looked like Fig. 8.4(a), then the first area would be as in Fig. 8.4 (b) and the second would be as in Fig. 8.4 (c).

Compute the ratio of these two areas, i.e:

$$R = \text{(Shared area)/(Total area)}$$

This number is an 'index' of something. Devise a name for that index and give the motivation for that choice.

Answers

My calculations led to a shared area (A_s) of about 65 square units and to a total area (A_t) of approximately 147.5 square units. The ratio R should be around 0.44.

The names given to this index should reflect the type of analysis a student is trying to build. Examples are index of 'stability of standards,' of 'impetus to publish,' of 'normality,' of 'persisting standards,' of 'publication non-proliferation,' of 'adequate and average performance,' of 'fundamental

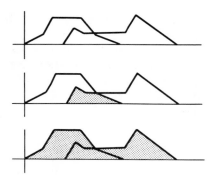

FIG. 8.4 *Example approximations of distribution polygons for samples I and II.*

research,' of 'paradigmatic research' (apparently producing less publications), of 'non-paradigmatic research' (again, apparently producing less publications). Given some justification, a wide variety of names for the index will do.

Properly understood, the flippant justification 'you asked for it' is exactly right.

QUESTION 8

Compute the variance (s^2), the standard deviation (s), and $(3/2)s$ for subsamples I and II. How do you explain the differences or similarities between the calculated values?

Answers

When used as a descriptive measure of a sample, the variance is often computed by taking the average of the squared differences of the individual scores from the mean. A formula for its computation is:

$$s^2 = \frac{\sum\limits_{i=1}^{N} (x_i - \bar{x})^2}{N}$$

although there are other formulae that make the calculation easier for the given tables. (As an estimate of the population variance, the sample variance is a test statistic and is more properly computed by dividing by $N-1$ in the formula above rather than N, in this way becoming a better (unbiased) estimate of the population parameter.) The standard deviation is the positive square root of the variance. (As an estimate, however, both s and $(\sqrt{N}/\sqrt{N-1})s$ are biased.) The variance is a measure of dispersion of the 'data' around the mean – a relatively small value would indicate that the individual scores (number of publications for the individual faculty members) cluster close to the mean; a large value would indicate the opposite. The standard deviation again reflects this dispersion, but its importance comes from its usefulness for computing probabilities on certain tabled probability distributions.

Using the formula given above, the approximate answers for the question are:

$$\text{Subsample I:} \; s^2 = 4.68 \quad s = 2.2 \quad (3/2)s = 3.3$$
$$\text{Subsample II:} \; s^2 = 7.95 \quad s = 2.8 \quad (3/2)s = 4.2$$

Since the variance is a measure of how close the individual scores cluster about the mean of a distribution, a comparison of the calculated values indicates a greater homogeneity of the number of publications for the faculty tenured in the 1960s. Again, explanations for this can vary widely. The change can be attributed to the effects of stress and the reaction to uncertainty about tenure standards – thus, to a non-stabilized working environment – or to changing standards concerning either numerically more publications or publications of greater quality; to increasing specialization and the accelerated growth of new subfields; to the importance attached to and relative time devoted to teaching; to a deterioration of quality controls, etc.

QUESTION 9

Compute the actual percentage of cases within one standard deviation and within 3/2 standard deviations from the mean for subsamples I and II. How do you explain these differences?

Solution

Table 8.7

	s	(*3/2*)s
Subsample I	74%	88%
Subsample II	65%	87.5%

As with the difference in the variance between the two subsamples, these percentages, shown in Table 8.7, indicate a greater homogeneity of the scores for the faculty tenured in the 1960s. The fact that roughly the same percentage occurs within (3/2)s for both subsamples might be interpreted to mean that some social regulation still exists for the faculty tenured later. An alternative interpretation is that the previous standards were artifically imposed.

QUESTION 10

Later in the [statistics] course we will examine methods of testing the (null) hypothesis that the discrepancy found in our sample means is the result of the samples' random selection and that the means in the actual populations – the faculty tenured in the 1960s and those in the 1970s at the universities examined – are equal. Per the espoused social science methodology, this hypothesis would have to be framed prior to the sampling or, at least, prior to any examination of the 'data.' In our exercise, the sampling distribution of differences in sample means is the 'student's t distribution.' Using the following formulae, compute a t-score and the degrees of freedom.[4]

$$t = \frac{|\bar{x}_I - \bar{x}_{II}|}{\hat{\sigma}_{\bar{x}_I - \bar{x}_{II}}}$$

$$\text{Degrees of freedom} = \frac{\left(\dfrac{S_I^2}{N_I - 1} + \dfrac{S_{II}^2}{N_{II} - 1}\right)^2}{\left(\dfrac{S_I^2}{N_I - 1}\right)^2 \left(\dfrac{1}{N_I + 1}\right) + \left(\dfrac{S_{II}^2}{N_{II} - 1}\right)^2 \left(\dfrac{1}{N_{II} + 1}\right)} - 2$$

where:

$$\hat{\sigma}_{\bar{x}_I - \bar{x}_{II}} = \sqrt{\frac{S_I^2}{N_I - 1} + \frac{S_{II}^2}{N_{II} - 1}}$$

Solution

$$\hat{\sigma}_{\bar{x}_I - \bar{x}_{II}} \approx 0.55$$
$$t \approx 3.64$$
$$\text{Degrees of freedom} \approx 73$$

The values inside the partial table, Table 8.8,[4] are t-scores. The values at the top of the table are the probabilities of getting that score, or greater, based on random sampling. If the means were really equal in the population, those numbers give the probability of getting your t-score or greater on the basis of random sampling. There is a choice of whether or not you are using a 'one-tailed' or 'two-tailed' test, and this depends on whether or not a direction (either increasing or decreasing average number of publications) in the difference in means had been predicted before you had conducted the test. The probabilities at the top of the table are called 'significance levels.'

QUESTION 11

Decide if you want to use a one-tailed or two-tailed test. Making the test as stringent as possible, place the t-score you calculated in the table in the row for the approximate degrees of freedom. Find the greatest possible significance level for your result. If your computations lead you to a value not on Table 8.8, use the table for the t-distribution in your text. Give the degrees of freedom you used and the significance level of your t-score, the 'test statistic.'

Table 8.8

Degrees of Freedom	Level of significance for a one-tailed test					
	0.10	0.05	0.025	0.01	0.005	0.0005
	Level of significance for a two-tailed test					
	0.20	*0.10*	*0.05*	*0.02*	*0.01*	*0.001*
30	1.310	1.697	2.042	2.457	2.750	3.646
40	1.303	1.684	2.021	2.423	2.704	3.551
60	1.296	1.671	2.000	2.390	2.660	3.460
120	1.289	1.658	1.980	2.358	2.617	3.373

Original source: Table III of Fisher and Yates, *Statistical Tables for Biological, Agricultural and Medical Research*, published by Longman Group Ltd, London (1974) 6th edition (previously published by Oliver and Boyd Ltd, Edinburgh) and by permission of the authors and publishers.

Solution

Using sixty degrees of freedom and a one-tailed test, the test statistic $t = 3.64$ is significant at the 0.0005 level. For a two-tailed test the significance level would be 0.001.

QUESTION 12

Table 8.9 gives the average number per year of 'qualified candidates' for each tenure track position in a number of sociology departments, not necessarily the ones used for our previous sample. 'Qualified candidates' is an index similar to 'number of publications.'

Table 8.9

Year	Average number of qualified candidates
1958	11.0
1959	10.5
1960	11.5
1961	12.0
1962	13.3
1963	14.8
1964	20.2
1965	17.0
1966	17.6
1967	19.0
1968	21.9
1969	25.2
1970	32.0
1971	28.3
1972	30.6
1973	35.1

Draw a graph to represent this 'data.'

A statistics exercise

Solution

See Fig. 8.5.

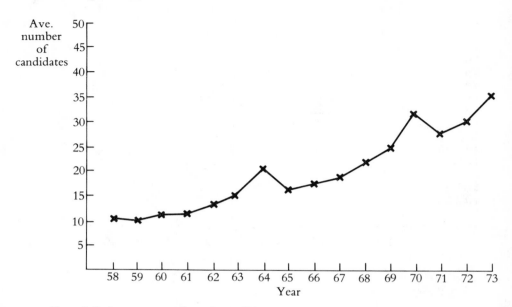

FIG. 8.5 *Average number of candidates per year.*

QUESTION 13

Add a column to Table 8.9, accurate to one decimal place, in which you compute the percent change per year in the average number of 'qualified candidates.' Sketch a graph for the percent change showing only the approximate shape of the graph.

Solution

See Table 8.10 and Fig. 8.6.

QUESTION 14

Do your answers to question 12 and 13 suggest a reason for the (conjectured) difference in the average number of publications between the two subsamples? If so, what is it? If not, why not?

Answers

Some possible answers are as follows.
1 There is increasing competition for faculty positions. In order to be tenured, faculty must demonstrate their qualifications for such a decision.

Table 8.10

Year	Percent change
1958	x
1959	− 4.5
1960	9.5
1961	4.4
1962	10.8
1963	11.3
1964	36.8
1965	−15.8
1966	3.5
1967	8.0
1968	15.2
1969	15.0
1970	27.0
1971	−11.6
1972	8.2
1973	14.7

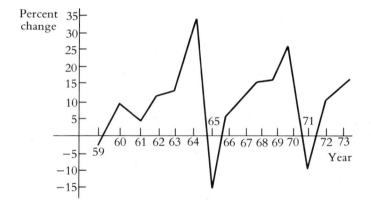

FIG. 8.6 *Percentage change in average number of candidates.*

2 The increased number of qualified applicants indicates that universities are able to select the very best scholars.
3 Both the increasing number of applicants and the cyclic rate of their increase produce uncertainty in young faculty concerning their tenure. In the attempt to control their fate, they respond by writing more.

A rather stale reason why the new material does not explain the difference in publication numbers is that there are technical, methodological problems in applying the new 'data' to the previous sample. Changes in the academic community – both the increasing professionalization of the faculty and the increasing number of students – could explain both the original tables and the

43

new ones. Similarly, the development of new subfields and the growth of scientific knowledge could explain the increasing number of job candidates and the increase in number of publications. The cyclic change could be a reflection of continually increasing standards, both for hiring new faculty and for tenure decisions. On the other hand, another explanation is that there no longer are any real standards of quality (perhaps because of intense specialization), so there are more job candidates and therefore more 'qualified' job candidates. A slight variation on this argument is that, because of the deterioration of standards, emphasis is placed on numbers of publications so as to fulfill extrinsic, university-wide accounting practices that are used to measure serious scholarly achievement and prevent, or maintain, discriminatory hiring practices.

QUESTION 15

Rephrase what you wrote in problem 14 as a hypothesis or group of hypotheses.

Answer

I leave an enumeration of possibilities to the reader. One possibility is: 'As competition increases, the professors who are tenured are both more qualified and work harder. Thus, more generally: 'As competition increases, both production and quality of production increase.' (?)

QUESTION 16

Briefly suggest some relationships, variables, or statistical information you might want or need to examine further your hypothesis(es); that is, sketch some method for addressing the issues raised by your analysis.

Answers

If the student said that the 'younger' faculty were more qualified than the 'older' faculty, developing some procedure to check if this were so – perhaps devising a measure based on the number of times a professor's publications are cited in certain journals – would seem appropriate. Taking a sample of those faculty who, after six years of residence, were not tenured might permit one to see if the characteristics of that population differed from the characteristics of the population that was.

The professors whose publication scores fell in either of the tails of the two polygons are candidates for closer inspection. Are the faculty with relatively higher numbers of publications 'high achievers' or is the quality of their work poor? How could this be measured? What about the 'low achievers'? Is there any regularity in the circumstances of their tenure or were their tenure decisions based on idiosyncracies of the individuals involved? Does that idiosyncratic character justify treating them as a distinct group or 'production cohort'? Questions about the raising of performance standards can lead to the suggestion of interviewing department chairpeople. Perhaps a battery of tests of hypotheses is needed to eliminate possible explanations, other than the one the student developed while working through the exercise, that might explain the 'data.' Should the time when faculty members actually published their papers be examined? How were their publications placed in the temporal course of their academic careers? Has there been a change in funding for sociologists? Checking the grants or fellowships tenured faculty received prior to tenure seems to be a good suggestion. Should the publication histories of different yearly cohorts of new faculty be compared? Is there a connection between the members of the faculty who published more than the others and the cyclic character of the percent change in qualified job candidates? Were the most prolific writers hired in years of 'peak competition'? Etc., etc.

QUESTION 17 (EXTRA CREDIT)

Think of what you have done in this exercise as developing a serious dissertation or grant proposal in sociology, except that now you should become skeptical about the methods and reasoning that you used. What is suspicious about what you did in the exercise? Could you have done something differently?

Answer

In general, students' imaginations and the time constraints that the students work under had been sorely tested. The students did the exercise in such a way as to get an adequate grade on it. This is comparable to the ways professional sociologists work to produce publishable papers or obtain grants. That the exercise or research could have been done differently, or that their own practical methods might merit serious examination, is exactly the opposite of what the students, or professionals, are trying to achieve through them. Those practices, partially available through the reading of their papers, are the observed and recognized grounds for the adequacy of their results.

Other than flippancy and invective, the answers one gets to this question tend to be wild-eyed conjectures – the groping search for something that could possibly be otherwise than the way the student said it was – or the type of methodological reflections that fill the sociological literature – the probing of proper statistical procedures, considerations of 'scientific' methods, or principled objections based on alternative methodologies. Those students who considered 'What if the research had been conducted differently?' and did not simply cite methodological precepts or alternative philosophies of practical action, ingenenuously discovering that there was something 'funny' about what they did – the arbitrary picking of faculty cohorts and the measures of performance, of extracting, interpreting, and manipulating numerical indices – began to discover, for themselves, something interesting about sociological praxis.

This is the point that I tried to make. Not only could the students have done things differently, but the 'data' on which the exercise was based could have been produced differently as well. Different faculty cohorts could have been chosen. I could have divided the array of numbers differently; different measures of numbers of publications could have been devised; completely different sets of 'data' could have been generated using different indices. The 'population' was not necessarily a production cohort, in the sense that its members produced the regularities of practical action that were being examined and analyzed, but a produced feature and artifact of the research. Different methods of inquiry could have produced completely different 'data' and completely different 'results.'

The students tried, and sociologists try, to control this variability of method and interpretation. That was what the students were doing when they used the material placed later in the exercise to review, criticize, reconstruct, and substantiate what they had previously written. Using more refined methods, a researcher could examine a range of different cohorts, build multiple indicators of 'performance' and compare them for their reliability, and use more sophisticated mathematical procedures.

The difficult point to make is that, through all this, something remains the same – the need for just these procedures. Didn't the students find the need for those refinements in the ellipses of their arguments? The arguments that the students constructed about the 'data' and the 'populations' had only a practical adequacy. They were adequate for the purposes and tasks at hand, like getting a grade or, for the professional, producing the publishable article needed to support tenure candidacy. Students and professionals both recognize this. It is a characteristic and accountable feature of their work. All the refinements that could be introduced, whether or not understood as the attempt to gain deeper access to a phenomenon of interest, therein and simultaneously are the attempts to turn the practical adequacy of their lived-work into an objective, disengaged demonstration of a 'true' finding. Yet every attempt that is made to repair this 'deficiency' – the recognized practical character of their findings – reincorporates the same things that produced it in the first place. The findings would always retain their practical, and their recognized practical, adequacy for the task-at-hand. The new results would need to be repaired with further arguments, with further refinements of the researcher's methods.

In spite of this, the exercise or the paper is completed. The demonstration of the various different arguments that could be documented through the exercise – the 'impossibility' of doing it – only sets in relief the fact that it was completed. The work of doing the exercise was practical through and through; the students' construction of their documented arguments was a hopelessly practical enterprise. The exercise's completion, and the cogency of the students' arguments, were practical accomplishments. How was this done?

When I reviewed the exercise, I illustrated the diversity of the answers that could be given and the diversity of arguments that could be justified and documented using the same extracted accounting procedures. When the students were working through the exercise, they did not give that range of 'answers.' Over the course of the exercise, they built a singular interpretation of the 'data' with qualifying remarks and fringes of noted inexactitudes and uncertainties. They realized that there were other possible 'real' or imaginable explanations, but they reasoned about them and discarded them as distractions from their practical tasks. Even if the exercise was done disingenuously – as something to be completed only for the grade they would receive – the students tried to build continuity and coherence in their answers. And once they started, they kept on going. What they had written before – the local and developing history of their own practices – provided the real-worldly circumstances of their further reasoning and writing. The students were led by the intrinsic logic of their own work to interpret their work in the ways that they did.

To see this, it may help to realize that all the 'data' was fictitious and that, in all probability, the students knew nothing about the intimate details of the tenure process. The point of the last question is that this made no difference. After constructing the polygons for the two subsamples, the polygons themselves had accountable features. Why, for example, was some professor tenured when she had published only 'one' article? The reasons that were offered – everyone must know that that professor is brilliant, the paper reported a great discovery, or she must be an exceptional instructor – interpret and explain the remarkable features of the polygon in terms of the imagined practices of the cohort or social environment that could have produced them. From within the work of completing the exercise, what the students did seemed to most of them to be completely reasonable. It was reasonable, and that is the interesting and bewildering thing about it.

What could be more natural than labeling the tables and graphs? Yet, labeling them makes them into a provisional explanation for the distinction that the labels themselves offer. The tables and graphs become documentation for something that has not yet been exhibited and, by being this, they provide the grounds for their exegesis. The graphs come to exhibit a yet unarticulated difference between the 'old regime' and the 'new' one or between 'scholars' and 'professionals.' Who knows what sociologists' tables and mathematical procedures would be about, as worldly descriptions, if sociologists were not forever labeling them, explaining them, and pictorially representing them? In turn, this activity becomes the source and aim of further explications and labels and arguments. The graphs and tables gain the sensibility and cogency that they have from within the work of providing for it.

The time and grading constraints that the students labored under were features of their work practices as well. Those constraints – like the constraints of limited funds, inexact knowledge, fallible procedures, and, above all, the need to be published – provided situated, local motives for some of the detailed things that the students did and did not do.

Over the course of the exercise, what the students did was build an increasingly articulated vision of a hidden, theorized order of practical action. They explained whatever regularities or orderlinesses they found *in* the 'data' in terms of how the academic community could be organized so as to produce them. The explanations that they offered – that there are changing standards of academic performance or that such standards have changed because of the increasing competition for job positions – are not necessarily observable features of the practices of tenure decisions. They describe a hidden order of those practices that the students' methods provided for as the 'real' order. This was itself a feature of the students' work. It is always a feature of work like theirs, and it is recognized as such. That this is so – that practitioners can conceive of no alternative research practice that would be different, and that they will not allow that such an alternative could exist – justifies, for them, the endless interpretation and reinterpretation of witnessable action in terms of what can only be interpretively seen when rendered through such a system of interpretation. That interpretive schema – the theorized order of practical action that produced the 'data' – was made practically available through the students' own practical methods of doing the exercise.

In any particular case, like the students' exercise, the particular interpretation that is given is practically justified through the use of the apparently disengaged accounting practices that comprise the mathematical procedures of sociology's taught and espoused, extracted methodologies. It is seen by the production cohort – the researchers – as a practical justification, a justification for the purposes and tasks at hand.

The relationship between these accounting procedures and sociologists' work practices is quite complex. The accounting procedures are themselves part of those work practices. At the same time, they are produced as a practically, but only practically, disengaged methodology. For the students in the class, in that the class was on statistical methods, I thought it enough to say that the existence of those articulated and continually refined accounting procedures – the so-called 'methods' of scientific sociology – allows sociologists, on every occasion, to treat the analysis of practical action and its orderlinesses – the problem of social order – as an engineering problem. They can build models and test them, they can justify the interpretation of those models in terms of practical action, they can question someone else's 'methods' and endlessly refine their own. Like an engineering problem, such as the construction of models of freeway traffic flow, the relative stability of the unexamined practices whereby the members of the ordinary society produce and manage their everyday affairs – including and particularly the relative stability of the practices of the investigator as a competent professional –

allows the sociologist to speak about those practices *as if* they filled their models and their interpretations of them.

The extractable methodologies of professional sociology gave to the students' work in completing the assignment its practical objectivity – its objectivity for the purposes of the exercise – and that is their point. The fact that the students' *arguments* were getting somewhere over the course of the exercise – that the signposts they had planted were getting clearer – led the students to believe they were really on their way somewhere after all. For the sociologist, this is the practical proof that this is so. This is what their 'beliefs' and 'confidence' and 'hopes' consist of.

The preceding exercise was designed to teach beginning students the practice of sociology's mathematical methods – heuristically, how mathematical methods are used in the course of professionally conducted inquiries. In doing so, it also offered those practices for examination as their own phenomenon. It attempts to teach how sociologists' work practices produce, and are used to produce, a practically adequate, practically objective, theorized regularity of practical action. It begins to show how those work practices are used to build an objective description of 'what is *really* going on.'

The last question of the assignment was added to see what the students did with it, as a reflection of my own interests, and to provide the grounds for introducing material that I thought the students might find interesting as well. In a class on 'research methods' this same exercise can be used as the basis of an introductory lecture on ethnomethodology. The outline of the next chapter was taken from my preparation notes.

Chapter 9
An introductory lecture on ethnomethodology

(This chapter is based on the exercise in Chapter 8.)

The last exercise that you did was designed to show how some of the methods of social science are used as part of a sociological investigation. Those 'methods' are based on statements such as the following.

In order to generalize from a sample to a population, the sample has to be randomly selected. If, for example, we had selected only people we knew or people for whom we could obtain the necessary information, that would have introduced a possible bias into our sample and our results. You computed various statistics like the mean and t-score; you calculated a test statistic. You should know what a test of hypotheses means and the probability concepts that are involved, and distinguish these from an interpretation of a test result. To test a hypothesis, you should frame that hypothesis and a possible 'direction' for the test before you begin to examine the 'data.' Otherwise, you would be using what you knew about the sample to make it seem as if you had conducted a test. In order to conduct the test in the exercise, you needed to use the t-distribution because the sizes of our samples indicated that both the estimate of the population variance and the difference in means had to be treated as random variables. The 'data' that is used in such a study should be carefully procured. We might not have been able to list all the professors in the population and, for various reasons, we might have had to eliminate some of the faculty from the sample. Indices for the 'number of publications' and for 'qualified job candidates' need to be carefully constructed. You should know not to assume a causal relationship because a measure of association you obtain is statistically significant. And, superimposed on all this, there is a philosophy of social science, often attributed to Durkheim, regarding the legitimacy of using these statistical procedures at all.

All these things are part of the 'methodology of social science.' They are the things that this course is supposed to be about. For the purposes of this lecture I am going to refer to these things as 'purported methods' or 'disengaged accounting procedures' or 'methods' in quotation marks. In this lecture I want to distinguish those things from the actual practices that are used in the course of conducting social science inquiries. I'll call these actual practices 'actual practices' or 'methods' or simply 'the things the researchers actually do.' Some of you may think that if research is conducted in accordance with a proper, disengaged methodology or accounting practice, that accounting practice is an adequate description of the methods that were actually used. You might think that there is no discrepancy between them. I think that there is; I think you know from your own experience that there is. But for those of you who cannot see it, this lecture is simply not for you. That doesn't mean I won't hold you responsible for sitting there and acting like you are listening and taking notes.

At the end of the last lecture, after I reviewed the exercise, I pointed out that it was possible to examine the whole exercise – what you did as well as and including your use of extractable mathematical methods and accounting procedures – as one object, sociological praxis, the actual methods sociologists use. As an example, at the beginning of the exercise you offered a reason for a population to produce a measured difference in samples taken from it. Over the course of the exercise you used the additional information you were given and sociologists' mathematical methods to develop your reasoning, to articulate the causes or work practices of the population that could have produced that 'data.' You used those disengaged methods to substantiate your reflections and arguments. If you found that your initial explanation did not fit the material that came later – perhaps because you thought that the exercise was a puzzle and that there was a correct solution – some of you went back and modified what you had done before. My hunch is that most of you developed a more finely-textured argument that preserved what you had previously written and brought the new material into its compass. I want to suggest to you that you found nothing extraordinary in that type of work and reasoning; in fact, it seemed very ordinary to you. It *was* ordinary. I don't mean that what some of you came up with wasn't bright and ingenious – it was – but that the methods and type of reasoning you used were familiar to both me and you.

When some of you come to complain about your grade, you will try to embed and elaborate what you wrote in very ordinary reasoning and try to show from within that reasoning how your answers should be properly interpreted. Sometimes the 'gaps' in your arguments are very interesting and instructive, and I try to imagine what social processes you envisioned such that your argument or reasoning was obvious from that perspective. That is something you did as well to justify what you had done before and explain new aspects of the exercise.

What we have been looking at so far in this course is the methodology of social science – how to compare various statistics, how to measure things, some of the concerns you should have in constructing indicators, how to check their reliability, how to analyze various tables of 'data,' and how all these procedures are justified. These things make up the traditional conception of methods; these are the traditional things taught as methods. This is just what we have been doing. What I want to propose today is that those disengaged methods provide a system of relevancies for an inquiry and an accounting procedure for what is actually done. Social science inquiries are performed in such a way as to be in accountable accord with that methodology. They are reinterpreted afterward so that they will be. These are not the actual methods that a researcher uses, the observable and observed things that you did, but they do come to be embedded in those practical methods as well. In fact, the reason some of you might think that the distinction between 'disengaged methods' and 'actual practice' is artificial is that social science inquiries are conducted and described in ways that make those disengaged procedures into practically adequate accounts of the researchers' actual practices. In this way, the adequacy of the disengaged account is an achievement of the things that the researcher is doing.

Since I have already used the word 'disengaged' quite a bit, I should tell you what I mean by it. The 'methods' that we have been discussing, like hypothesis testing and constructing social indicators, are supposed to be separate from the particular investigation in which a researcher is engaged. They are not supposed to have anything to do with the particular content of the research. They apply to investigations of any number of substantively different social processes. The standard account is that they are abstract mathematical procedures that sociologists use to legitimate, support, and develop their reasoning and findings. The fact that these 'methods' are apparently disengaged from the particular things that the researcher is doing is what gives legitimacy to their use. That is the point of teaching 'research methods.'

Now I am saying that these 'methods' are only 'apparently' disengaged from the actual conduct of an inquiry, from sociologists' work practices. What could I mean?

When you did the exercise, you labeled the tables so that the tables could be seen to evince properties of the distinction that the labels made. You pictorially represented the tables so that you could interpret them. You treated indicators as if they were the things they were constructed to measure. We built in the justification for the use of statistical procedures through methods of sampling, although, had we actually done the sampling, you would have recognized the flawed or practical character of the way we did it. Sociologists would have stated the principal assumptions of the statistical test that they used, such as the assumption that the number of publications of the individual faculty members in the population is normally distributed. No one knows what this means in terms of the work practices of the population. If we really did check this assumption, it would be something like your looking at the frequency polygons and calling them normal distributions. Technically, the assumption allows the sociologist to assume that the estimated difference in means and the estimated variance are independent random variables. Practically, it allows them to use a statistical test that is both familiar and accessible to them. After distinguishing the statistical meaning of a test from its substantive interpretation, we continued to speak about the test in terms of substantial interpretation. We rely on our knowledge of performance evaluation – such as the relative weight given to different publications – to construct indicators.

Throughout all this, you and professionals know what you are doing. You recognized that you were interpreting organized displays of numbers and that the real world didn't have to be the way you argued that it was. And you used that recognition to reinterpret and evaluate and modify what you had done.

The point of all this is that the disengageable methodologies of social science are themselves part of the sociologists' practical methods. They are produced to be extractable from them. They are built within those practical, situated methods as an accountable feature of the local practices and as an accounting procedure for them. Through this type of work the real society – how tenure decisions are made – is turned into a society disengaged from the work people do to produce it. The problems of documenting and studying the real society's orderlinesses – the problem of social order – is turned into an external problem. By using appropriate 'methods' of proper research, the investigator is allowed to theorize about, document, and analyze the produced orderlinesses of the social world in disregard for the detailed ways in which society is locally producing, *in situ*, those orderlinesses. The purported 'methods' and mathematical procedures are intended and used by sociologists to give their research its practical objectivity. They are used by the researcher to make herself into an apparently disengaged, objective observer of an equally disengaged, objective social world.

Instead of pursuing this, let us simply look at some of the things you did in the exercise. You used sociological 'methods' to help build an interpretation of social action that would explain a documented regularity of it – that professors are publishing more, now, prior to tenure, than their predecessors were. You gave names to different collections of numbers like 'old faculty'/'new faculty' or 'old generation'/'new generation.' You put titles on tables, you made graphs, you computed a test statistic, you compared one set of numbers to another aided by the use of graphs.

What you were doing was building into your work the real-worldly aspects of the things to be discovered, documented, conjectured, and argued about those arrays of numbers. Having constructed a graph, you could explain a point on it as the description of particular people. The 'young' faculty member who was tenured with 'one' publication was probably 'brilliant' or a 'political hustler' or a 'supplier of grant funds.' Having labeled a table, you used the table to document what was consequential about the label. You saw a graph as having a repeating pattern and then used that to describe a social process as being cyclic. The do's and don'ts of the purported 'methods' gave the exercise the air of its being a technical enterprise. In fact, they are what makes the enterprise technical; they are what is technical about it. That technicality did not have to do with the actual details of how tenure decisions are made. Instead, the real world was built into the exercise as a developing and documented vision of a hidden, theorized order of tenuring practices. 'These are the hidden or real causes for the produced orderlinesses of the "data." ' 'This is the unseen casual thing happening in tenure decisions.'

If we look back at the exercise, we see that both the capital letter methods and the little methods you used to complete it – the way you drew and labeled the graphs, the way you reasoned about them, the way you made sure that your developing argument was consistent, the ways you found it was inconsistent or hypothetical – all these things provided the cogency of what you were doing. They provided the next thing to be investigated or explained. They were all natural in the sense that they were just part of your own organizational work in completing the exercise. There was no conflict between the big methods and the little ones – the big ones were naturally fitted into the things you were doing. It was all very ordinary, and you produced your argument as something ordinary so that it could be seen as an explanation of what was really making the documented difference between the two subsamples. Besides the little problems involved in completing the exercise, there were no other problems. I did not ask you to write your answers in Sanskrit. You might have seen the exercise as being 'too much,' but it was not impossible.

The point is that the 'data' in the exercise was not really analyzed in the sense of being examined in terms of the practices that make up tenure decisions. Instead, an interpretation was built from it. The methodology – what is supposed to be explicitly taught in a course on 'research methods' – was retained throughout as a disengaged accounting procedure justifying your work. All the time you recognized that you were interpreting and imagining the whole thing. You did all this without ever examining, or needing to examine, the real-world settings that produced the 'data' you were interpreting.

The ethnomethodologist would view this exercise as a miniature of sociological praxis. There is a tendency for us to trivialize what we do, to think that real sociology is going on somewhere else. Professional arguments may be more technically involved, but the ethnomethodologist would say that the type of work you were doing was the type of work professionals do. That should make you pretty happy. Ethnomethodologists are not directly interested in sociologists' purported methods. They are interested in the actual methods people use to produce the orderlinesses of the social world. They are interested in the methods you used to make the exercise into a real world analysis, into a study of what really caused the difference in publication rates. The big methods helped you along. As your argument became clearer, and as the relevance of the big methods became clearer from within your work, it seemed as if the real world was becoming clearer as well. The clarity of your argument made you feel that you were really on your way.

From an ethnomethodological perspective, we could re-examine the topics of this course:

Interviewing
Coding
Sampling

Social-psychological tests
Data analysis
Indicators

Harold Garfinkel was the founder of ethnomethodology. Borrowing from the phenomenologists, he introduced the device of bracketing. What he did was to put brackets about such topics:

[Interviewing]
[Coding]
[Sampling]
[Social-psychological tests]
[Data analysis]
[Indicators]

We could add some more:

[Observing]
[Describing]
[Theorizing]

His point was that, rather than talking about them in the idealized way that we have, we should see them as activities. The recommendation was to study the work of 'coding,' the work of 'hypothesis testing,' and to discover how these things get done so as to be the things that they accountably are. The brackets serve as a reminder of the social processes and organized settings we are referring to when we speak of [interviewing] and [coding]. The descriptive appropriateness of the word or words inside the brackets for the activities they name is a practical achievement of that social – or organizational – work.

The lived-work, or the lived organizational work, of such ordinary, mundane activities makes up the witnessed orderlinesses of the social world, just as the lived-work of completing the exercise made up the orderliness of the exercise for you. The ethnomethodological point is that by studying the work of producing social things like a properly constructed social indicator – that is, by studying [indicators] – one begins to discover a domain of phenomena that provides for and makes up sociology's topics and methods. Ethnomethodologists refer to this domain as that of practical action and practical reasoning.

Having introduced a notational device, we might as well put it to work. When you think of 'social order,' you might think of the contrast with 'social disorder' or 'social unrest.' This is not quite the way it is used in sociology. Social 'disorder' – like race riots – is viewed as an order phenomenon. The sociologist tries to document or explain the regularities of such occurrences, including the regularities of their change. By the term 'social order' the ethnomethodologist refers as well to things like:

[Queues]
[Traffic flow]
[*Your* seat in class]
[Greetings]

[Questions]
[Lectures]
[Walking together]
[A test of hypotheses]
[Completing an exercise]

The fact that you can name these things when you see or do them is tied to the witnessed orderliness of the produced social events or objects. They are produced as the things that they are seen practically to be. As Garfinkel might say, the social order is omnipresent, familiar, vulgarly available, practically observable and observed, practically objective, available in and as the lived-details of the real world. The idea of speaking about practical action and practical reasoning is that they are the work of producing social objects. They are practical in that sense – they are the things we do to get the job done, to build the observable and observed orderlinesses of the social world. That is what these orderlinesses consist of – practical action and practical reasoning.

For ethnomethodologists and sociologists alike, the investigation and analysis of, theorizing about, and accounting for the observed or documented regularities of practical action make up the 'problem of social order.' Ethnomethodologists study the problem of social order as a production problem. They view the production of the ordinary real society as members' work. In fact, the people producing the local orderlinesses of the social world – a social object's production cohort – see, witness, depend on, and ignore the work of their production. That they ignore it is something interesting about practical action and reasoning. [Asking a question] is just [asking a question]. And the ordinariness of [asking a question] is part of [asking a question]. It is a produced ordinariness; the ordinariness of the production of the social event – the [question] – is an organizational feature of it. In a sense, a question is produced so as to get the conversation 'done,' so as not to be problematic, so that you can hear the particular thing the question is asking and respond to it. It is produced so as not to raise questions about its own work.

Pretty much, ethnomethodologists study very localized settings like [queues], [constructing social indicators], and [questions]. One reason they might give is that that is what the social order – the mundane society – looks like. Another reason is that practical action and practical reasoning are always embodied in their living effacements. The ethnomethodologist tries to study them *in concretia* without trading on properties of the domain to theorize about it. I think that there is another reason as well. It is somewhat different from what we, or I, have been talking about. Ethnomethodologists see practical action and practical reasoning – the work of producing the observed and accountable orderlinesses of the social world – as social science's fundamental phenomena. What they want to do is make discoveries about this domain. Because that domain is always embodied in its detailed, living effacements, they study settings that provide detailed, technical access to it.

For the ethnomethodologist, the production of social order is both unavoidable and a hopelessly situated, local accomplishment. There is no relief from it or disengaged place to observe it from. The problems for analysis that result are extreme. What I would like to suggest, however, is that this lack of a disengaged, objective perspective is itself a finding about practical action and reasoning. It is a problem for members of a social object's production cohort, not just for ethnomethodologists. Yet, in spite of this, or against this problematic background, the social object is produced. Its accomplishment is a practical achievement, the production cohort recognizes it as such, and they work to maintain it.

A criticism of ethnomethodology is that, because there is no Archimedian position for the observer or analyst, someone could do an ethno-study of an ethno-study, and an ethno-study of that, and an ethno-study of that. . . But an ethnomethodologist intends the statement regarding the lack of an Archimedian position to be a finding and a research recommendation about the phenomenal domain. She would put 'brackets' around that criticism. Let me show you what I mean.

When I said 'an ethno-study of an ethno-study' once, I moved my hand in a small circle away from my body and back toward it, and I nodded my head in synchrony with that movement and my words; when I said it again, I repeated those actions; when I said it again, I did the same thing, and then I paused, holding my hand and my head in a fixed position stopping the motion. Then I made the gestures one more time. What I showed you was that I could keep on moving my hands and repeating what I had said. I was literally stopping myself from doing it. I think that's what you saw and heard, isn't it? That makes up the practical achievement of practically showing that there is an infinite regress. Ethnomethodologists are no better off than we are. So even if we could do otherwise, we're right to be doing sociology just the way we are. That's the point of the little drama.

The person who voices this criticism generally has no intention of doing an 'ethnomethodological study of ethnomethodology.' She uses properties of the domain of practical action and reasoning – the practices of ordinary conversation and natural theorizing – to argue the pointlessness of doing so and, therein, to justify her continuing to work in the ways she always has. She knows the practical character of her work and insists that it must be the same for ethnomethodologists. So it is. The ethnomethodological claim is that that is sociology's fundamental phenomenon, and ethnomethodologists have attempted to study it both in and as their own work practices and in and as the work practices of others.

Because a production cohort recognizes – in the practical character of their ongoing activities – that there is no disengaged observational position, ethnomethodologists are always putting the words 'practical' and 'practically' before every other word they say. Something is 'practically objective' or a method is 'practically adequate.' Their point is that a production cohort recognizes that the objectivity of what they are doing is an objectivity for practical purposes, for the purposes of producing the social thing that they are producing. This doesn't mean that ethnomethodologists have found the Archimedian position. As I said, the problems for analysis that result are extreme. It means that a criticism of their methods is not so obvious. Very often when you attempt such a criticism, when you take up the details of their studies to criticize them, you find yourself doing ethnomethodology.

If we return to the exercise one last time, you might want to ask, 'All this is well and good, but still, isn't the increase in publication rate a result of increasing competition for academic positions?' or 'Isn't it caused by the implementation of new accounting procedures for professional performance?' You are more sophisticated than this and instead would probably say something like, 'There are a number of interrelated causal variables, competition is one of them, and it is a good predictor of increased publication rate.' This is a different kind of statement because it refers to the researcher's practices of inquiry. In any case, there are worse things to be saying behind someone's back.

To the idea that there really are real, hidden 'causes,' I think the ethnomethodologist might respond by saying that she is indifferent to that aspect of sociology. She is not interested – as an ethnomethodologist – in taking a position on some issue. She is interested in studying the ways in which – the practical methods through which – a sociologist builds or documents such an argument. She is interested in observable practice, in the ways an explanation or account or question is a feature of the organizational activity of which it is hopelessly a part. The hidden order of the social world is simply inaccessible, always being made practically available from within a naturally organized activity.

The ethnomethodologist wants to study how the society – or social order – is built from within the building of it. She views the larger structures of the social world as being locally produced and as, in fact, always witnessed and observed locally. She wants to investigate how the always, and only, locally available global structures of practical action are produced and exhibited locally, *in situ*, as global structures. That is the kind of thing that you were doing in the exercise. You built an argument for the hidden, real, global structure of tenuring practices. The documentation of such a global or objective order of practical action is what 'research methods' are all about. In this lecture, we began to look at those methods as themselves artful, local practices.

Chapter 10
The barbecue

If we summarize the earlier discussion of pedestrian traffic flow as showing that a method of analysis can document a regularity of practical action that is not intrinsic to the pedestrians' organizational activities, and if we summarize the statistics exercise as showing how a method of analysis can substantiate a developing vision of a hidden, theorized order of practical action, then the moral of this chapter is that a method of analysis can hide the lived-orderliness of a phenomenon that the use of that method was specifically intended to illuminate.

Some years ago I was a participant in a seminar on conversational analysis, a discipline directed to the examination of conversation as a naturally organized ordinary activity. At the time, the use of videotape recordings for the detailed study of social interaction was becoming the rage. The conversational analysts in the seminar were trying to incorporate visible action – like gestures and facial expressions – into their analyses. As I understood their efforts, they wanted to specify how facial expressions and body and hand gestures are, for co-conversationists, an integral part of the identifying, lived, organizational work of a conversation.

One day a videotape was offered to the seminar participants for their examination, and a provisional transcript of the verbal track, made by someone not present, was distributed. It was to be a working seminar – there was no planned instructional order to the discussion; the tape was relatively unexamined by everyone present, and the floor was opened for suggestions. In the visual segment with which we became concerned, two couples were having a picnic together. The husband of one of the couples (husband$_1$) was seated across the picnic table from the wife of the other couple (wife$_2$). The other husband (husband$_2$) and wife (wife$_1$) were away from the table, busy with the barbecue. Husband$_2$ approached the table from behind and to the left of husband$_1$ and asked a question. Husband$_1$ turned to look at his lap, and wife$_2$ occupied herself shooing an insect.

Prima facie, husband$_1$'s glance downward and scrutiny of his lap had nothing to do with the question that husband$_2$ had asked. The question that was raised for examination in the seminar was, if they were related, then how? In order to decide the issue, other questions were raised. There was a concern for precisely marking the point in the transcript at which husband$_1$'s head motion began – a very complicated issue in that an observed action is already an action in the midst of its production. There were problems hearing all the conversational details in the recording. The directedness of husband$_1$'s downward gaze became problematic, and the seminar members wondered whether or not he had something in his lap.

The outcome of this examination was inconclusive. It was decided that the verbal recording and the camera's angle and focus were inadequate to decide the issues that had been raised. This led to a discussion of the kind and quality of technology that was needed to study such occurrences – like having multiple cameras filming from different places. It led, as well, to the discussion of the methodological prerequisites for producing an adequate analysis. What detail and what kind of documentation were needed to demonstrate how the actions of husband$_1$ were positioned to fit into the produced structure of husband$_2$'s question? Did one need a more detailed transcript? Was a procedure for annotating action and positioning that annotation in the transcript a necessary prerequisite for finding the mutually elaborating structure of both men's actions?

In contrast to these considerations, the little drama on the videotape becomes intelligible with the addition of one preliminary remark. When two people hold each other's gaze too long, it becomes more than a passing glance. It can be, and often is, understood by the participants as an indication of sexual attraction. Husband$_1$ and wife$_2$ had looked too long in each other's eyes. They recognized that they were maintaining each other's gaze; they had not denied it either by turning away (Fig. 10.1).

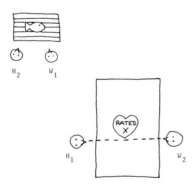

Fig. 10.1

When husband$_2$ came to the table, he had not necessarily seen that his wife and friend were looking into each other's eyes. The time it takes for actual participants to realize that they are doing this is extremely short; there was no indication on the tape that husband$_2$ had attended to it. But for his wife and friend, the sexuality of their deepening eye contact was an objective thing between them. That is what both recognized that they were doing together.

When husband$_2$ made his presence known by asking his question, they realized that he could see this too, not because he could, but because, for them, as the social object they were producing together, it was an objective thing to be seen. The turning of their eyes was the act of surprised lovers. That action not only stopped the production of the object by turning away the agents integral to its production; by giving their eyes other objects on which to produce a witnessably directed and held gaze – the mysterious thing in the lap, the bothersome insect – they attempted to make the held eye contact into just one of the many things that eyes linger on – other eyes. Neither had responded to the question by looking at the questioner, actions that betrayed their foul and guilty hearts. This was the missed orderliness of the witnessed drama on the videotape, a revealing episode of sin discovered (Fig. 10.2).

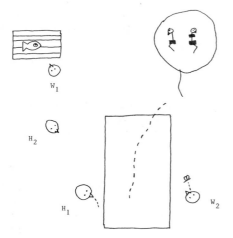

Fɪɢ. 10.2

For the ethnomethodologist, nothing critical to ethnomethodology rests on the interpretation of one videotape segment. What puzzled me was the methodological preoccupations of the seminar participants. They seemed to prefer discussing the need for further detail and documentation in order to make a case for there being anything of interest on the tape rather than using the tape to exploit its own possibilities, motivating the need for refining their own practices in their attempt to gain deeper access to the phenomenon being witnessed. Ironically, it is a phenomenon that is impossible, through the use of documenting records, to 'prove' is occurring, yet all of us know that it does occur.

The seminar members' concern for detail and documentation points to an equivalence between the seminar participants and the happy picnickers. For a local production cohort, producing a social object in such a way that it is practically observable, by them, as just that object is an ongoing, if ignored, concern. What detail and timing were needed to make husband$_1$'s and wife$_2$'s gazes into mutually recognized eye contact and, therein, into an objective, developing, deepening inquiry into their own and the other's motives for continuing it? Their turning away indicates that, for them, they had produced a witnessably objective social object – the liaison. What detail must a co-conversationist give to a question to make it hearable, for co-conversationists, as the particular thing that the question is questioning? What are the continuing and continually assessed actions of a pedestrian that produces for her fellow walkers her witnessable trajectory across and into the opposing current?

Ethnomethodologically, this is the research problem of understanding and elucidating the 'identifying detail' of a produced social object or social event – like eye contact or a question – as it is available to and produced by its production cohort over the course of its own production. For the analyst examining a setting not her own – like the seminar participants analyzing the videotape – this problem is translated into the problem of producing the detail needed to substantiate claims about the real-worldly things a production cohort is doing. The recognized practical character of the adequacy of their claims provides professional researchers with their endless tasks of turning that practical adequacy into an indubitable, 'objective' finding. This was the substance of the methodological reflections that arose in the seminar. The seminar members were concerned with the requirements of documenting the existence of some – and, therein, any – 'event' or 'thing.' By viewing the seminar members as a production cohort in their own right, their concern was with producing the identifying detail of their own practices that would allow them to advance real-worldly claims about what was happening on the tape. Their inability to produce that detail and to make a practically accountable argument about the real thing on the tape occasioned their examination of their own practices – translated into the inadequacies of the tape – so that, hopefully, they could produce such identifying detail, if not now, then later.

There is another equivalence between the filmed actions and the seminar. When I offered my understanding of what was happening on the videotape, the seminar leader treated it as being utterly inconsequential and unworthy of serious consideration. His dismissal was done in an off-handed manner. Was I so clearly wrong? Only much later did I realize that he, like the man on the tape, had been surprised by the witnessability of his 'sin.' By offering an interior coherence to the actions on the film, the new viewing – like the question husband$_2$ had asked – inadvertently made his illicit congress with the students in the seminar observable. His dismissal, his lack of interest, and his turning to new material was similar to the picnickers averting their eyes. By dismissing the alternative suggestion – by finding new things on which the eyes could fix their gaze – he used that dismissal to instruct the seminar in the propriety of the things that they were doing.

What was this illicit 'conspiracy' that bonded the members of the seminar to each other?

In itself, it does not concern conversational analysis, conversational analysts, or the seminar leader. It concerns the academic workplace. What occurred in the seminar occurs so regularly to ethnomethodologists that it has the status of being its own phenomenon. Its orderliness is a 'secret' story of academic research.

First, it involves the professional analyst's use of purportedly disengaged methods of analysis, whether they be the statistical methods of mathematically-oriented sociologists, the use of film documentation for ethnographers, or the use of detailed transcripts, repeated listenings to small portions of recorded utterances, and the use of 'known' structures – like an objective set of rules for conversational turn organization – to make claims and to document what is 'really' happening in some naturally organized activity. It does not concern the use of these 'methods' *per se*, but their use as 'methods' disengaged from the practitioners' work practices assuring the practical adequacy of those work practices and the 'findings' that are obtained through them. Second, one must understand that all of the 'problems' of analysis that we have been discussing – the recognized practical character of the adequacy of analysts' descriptions, the documentation of hidden, theorized orders of practical action, the missed orderliness of a phenomenon itself – are themselves technical order phenomena.

To make this transition, one ingredient must be added to the description of those 'problems.' One way of reading all the foregoing examples is that they describe ways in which a particular researcher attempted to analyze a naturally organized activity and the difficulties she encountered through her individual approach. The transformation that is needed is to understand that these problems are embedded in a researcher's own professionally competent work practices. She does not have the freedom to offer a description as an illustration of a particular point. The methods that she uses and the arguments that she builds are not a matter of choice. They are constrained by their being part of the work of producing, for colleagues, a practically adequate demonstration that something is the way the researcher says it is. The professional, discipline-based researcher conducts her research in such a way that her colleagues will see it as meritorious work, as producing practically objective findings. For her, the existence of the social object under examination is essentially tied to the professionally accountable methods of producing its accountably demonstrable features.

The primal scene that ethnomethodological analysis frequently makes apparent, entirely parallel to the situation captured on the videotape, *is* the identifying orderliness of the object that professional researchers – as a production cohort – are engaged in producing. That identifying orderliness is this: the preoccupying issue of their work is the production of the written and professionally published article.

The 'published article' refers not just to this self-named, projected, and projectively celebrated achievement, but to a style and organization of work practices. Everything the researcher does is directed to this end. Everything is directed toward the publication of practically accountable results. Everything. And by 'practically accountable results' one must understand that the production cohort is not only the immediate co-workers, but the professional colleagues who will read the paper to see, in the manner in which the research was conducted, that it reports a practically accountable finding, that they cannot discard it, and that they must treat it as part of the context of their own continuing inquiries and writings.

What is inadvertently heard in an ethnomethodological analysis is the denial of the adequacy of an analyst's technical proficiency as the manner in which a particular phenomenon of interest *must* be investigated. For the analyst, it must be that way in order to produce the publishable article reporting the practically adequate findings that were made available through those methods. However long it takes, it is the dream of her future, celebrated achievement – the published article – that sustains her and informs the minutest detail of her work practices. The uncovered sin is the fact that the seminar members, and academic researchers in general, all allow themselves to work that way, that they all recognize that that is what they are doing, and that they insist that that is the proper way collaborative research should be done. For a professional (social science) analyst to allow the possibility that she could act otherwise – that her work practices could be entirely different – especially in front of students, would turn her hopes and dreams, and her achievement of professional recognition, into a hollow prize indeed.

Although the discovering sciences are quite a different enterprise than the non-discovering ones, it is interesting to read a physicist's introductory comments to his book on theoretical physics.[1]

> There are, of course, very good reasons why the standard lecture course has evolved into its present form. First of all, physics and theoretical physics are not particularly easy subjects and it is important to set out the individual elements of the disciplines in as clear and systematic manner as possible. It is absolutely essential that all students acquire a very firm grounding in the basic techniques and concepts of physics. But we should not confuse this process with doing real physics. Lecture courses in physics and theoretical physics are basically 'five-finger' exercises and five-finger exercises bear little relation to a performance of the *Hammerklavier* sonata at the Royal Festival Hall. You are only doing physics and theoretical physics when the answers *really* matter – in other words, when your reputation as a scientist hangs upon being able to do physics correctly in a research context or, in more practical terms, when your ability to reason correctly determines whether you are employable or whether your research grant is renewed.

Chapter 11

Conversational practice

In studies of language and linguistic behavior it is now common to make the distinction, whose theoretical importance is attributed to Saussure, between language and speech. The examination of either depends on the fact that we have conversations with each other. As just one example, linguists ask, and know how to ask, questions, as we all do. They use and rely on the local, occasioned skills involved in doing so to collect, or to make up, examples of them. They then analyze those collections, again relying on the same conversational skills, to find their underlying or hidden structures. Throughout, the linguist depends on the relative stability of conversational practice to assure the accountable adequacy of her own work practices and the descriptiveness of her findings. Given linguists' practically accountable professional methods, the structures of questions that they 'find' and document are claimed to be objective, *a priori*, formal aspects of language or speech.[1]

When linguists actually compare the rendered structures of questions they have 'discovered' with conversational practice, they find, in and as the details of that practice, discrepancies between those details and their theoretical constructions. Therein, as a means of preserving and justifying their methods of analysis, a distinction is made between 'competence' and 'performance.' The idea is that co-conversationists know better (competence) than the way they speak (performance). In turn, the distinction is substantiated by the fact that co-conversationists undertake repair procedures during a conversation and that people correct 'ungrammatical' conversational constructions when taking a test designed to show this. But while the linguist examines the relationship between 'competence' and 'performance' through such repair and testing procedures, what repair and test behavior consist of as part of a naturally organized ordinary activity is never examined. Instead, the discrepancy between 'competence' and 'performance' is used as the grounds for further research and theorizing.

The inexactitudes of linguists' descriptions of 'performance' – as provided by their idealized models of 'competence' – is treated, by linguists, as a theoretical problem – that of explaining how conversationists imperfectly transform 'deep structures' in the attempt to fit them to their immediate conversational purposes, purposes that are themselves interpretive renderings of conversationists' lived-work. Through such professionally competent research practices, linguists turn real-world conversations into disembodied specters, something like the shadows of Plato's cave. In order to document the 'real,' i.e. hidden, orderlinesses of conversational events (like questions and questioning), linguistics has become the study of the structures of the mind, the theorized object that linguists need in order to have conversationists do the things that the linguists theorize co-conversationists must do in order to speak the way they claim conversationists speak. Throughout, linguists have consistently missed the fact that a conversation's production cohort produces and manages, *in situ*, as practical action and reasoning, the ordinary conversation's ordinary events that they eventually hope to explain.

In contrast to most current linguistic research, conversational analysis, whose origins lay in the collaboration of Harold Garfinkel and Harvey Sacks, is a discipline directed to the examination of conversation as a naturally organized activity. Although the distinction is commonly made between language and speech, conversational analysts took the distinction seriously. Co-conversationists' successful organization of a conversation – and, therein, that they are speaking meaningfully with each other – provides the genetic origins of both language and speech. That we can talk about language and speech, that we can analyze utterances such as questions, and that a correspondence between those analyses and conversational speech is assured through the practical methods of such analyses, are all based on the fact that we have, and are skilled in the practices of, ordinary conversations with each other.

What Sacks and his collaborators did was to make detailed transcripts of tape-recorded conversations. Rather than using a phonetic system to make the transcripts, they insisted on transcribing what was hearable on the tapes – the pauses, the slurs, the repeats, the 'incorrect' tenses, the overlaps, the stretched and emphasized 'syllables.' The revolutionary aspect of their work, however, was that, by using those transcripts in conjunction with the recordings, they attempted to discover what the hearable and heard, identifying conversational work of producing a conversation's ordinary events is for co-conversationists. They attempted to specify what a conversation consisted of, for co-conversationists, as practical action and practical reasoning. The orderlinesses of a conversation were seen as a problem in social order; the aim of the conversational analysts was to discover what, in their phenomenal lived-detail, those orderlinesses were and how they were locally produced.

As a means of introducing conversational analysis, this chapter examines a a part of a transcript, GST:2:2:19[2]. A double slash // in the transcript indicates the place at which the utterance of the following speaker interrupts the present one; the numbers in parentheses give the conversational seconds – counted to the pace of the recorded conversation – of a pause. Punctuation reflects a speaker's heard achievement, incorporating intonation and inflection, not a grammatical interpretation. Although linguists have become increasingly involved in the analysis of conversational materials, the reader might want to compare this transcript with the artificially constructed or extracted and manicured sentences that have been linguists' more traditional concern.

1 ROGER I–*I* been thinkina buildin a fallout shelter.
2 (1.0)
3 KEN hh
4 ROGER But I'd just throw parties th(hh)ere anywa(hh)ys hehh it'd be a fall
5 *in* shelte(h)r heh//hh
6 AL heh
7 KEN Hey –
8 (0.5)
9 AL heh
10 KEN Have you seen some a' these – fallout shelters?
11 ROGER Yeah, I've seen so::me
12 (1.0)
13 ROGER Be a // *nas*ty place tuh hide fro(h)m the // co(h)ps
14 KEN The lady –
15 KEN Well – // the lady up the street just–just had one put in? About
16 four days ago?
17 AL hehh hh hh hhh! ha
18 (DAN) Mm hm?
19 KEN And there's so // many –
20 ROGER An' she threw a house war//ming! hh!
21 KEN Waita minute
22 (   ) ((cough))
23 AL heh heh
24 KEN Waita minute
25 ROGER hh a // *bomb*! hehh hh hehh hh
26 KEN She's gotta *gun* in it.
27 KEN She's gotta gun hangin' there? And I said what's the gun for she said
28 in case any a' my *neigh*bors wanna come in. // Yuh know?

As conversational analysts' studies became increasingly refined, their transcripts reflected this, noting, for instance, greater intonational ranges, indicating in-breaths, and placing overlaps so that they were more clearly visible. By reorganizing the transcript above to highlight overlapping utterances, the repeated 'just–just' of Ken's fifth utterance (line 15) can be seen as a possible instance of a 'post-overlap hitch,' a documented regularity whose discovery, I believe, is due to Emanuel Schegloff.

15 KEN ⌊Well – ⌈the lady up the street just–just had one put in? About
17 AL   ⌊hehh hh hh hhh! ha

When co-conversationists compete in an overlap for a turn-at-talk, the one who 'wins' that turn will, with great regularity, repeat a portion of her utterance – the 'post-overlap hitch.' The examination of how Ken's 'just–just' is a 'post-overlap hitch' provides this *Guide*'s first introduction to conversational analysis.

To begin, we must first establish that, in line 15, Ken is, in fact, competing for the current turn-at-talk. As early as Ken's first utterance in line 3, more pointedly in line 7, and in his question in line 10,

1 ROGER I–I been thinkina buildin a fallout shelter
2 (1.0)
3 KEN hh
4 ROGER But I'd just throw parties th(hh)ere anywa(hh)ys hehh it'd be a fall
5 *in* shelte(h)r heh ⌈hh
6 AL   ⌊heh
7 KEN Hey –
8 (0.5)
9 AL heh
10 KEN Have you seen some a' these – fallout shelters?

Ken is working to introduce the story whose point he tells in lines 26, 27, and 28:

KEN She's gotta *gun* in it.
KEN She's gotta gun hangin' there? And I said what's the gun for she said in case any a' my *neigh*bors wanna come in. ⌈Yuh know?

Ken begins the point of his asking 'have you seen some a' these – fallout shelters?' in line 15.

13 ROGER Be a ⌈*nasty* place tuh hide fro(h)m the ⌈co(h)ps
14,15 KEN   ⌊The lady –   ⌊Well –
    KEN ⌈the lady up the street just–just had one put in? About
17 AL ⌊hehh hh hh hhh! ha
16 KEN four days ago?
18 (DAN) Mm hm?
19 KEN And there's so ⌈many –
20 ROGER   ⌊An' she threw a house war ⌈ming! hh!
21 KEN   ⌊Waita minute

This turns Roger's 'funny' remarks into, for Ken, a subterfuge of conversational organization. There are really two turn structures that are being produced, and there is competition for which one will dominate.[3] In line 17 for example, Al responds to Roger's utterance in line 13 – 'be a *nasty* place tuh hide fro(h)m the co(h)ps' – with a conversationally appropriate 'next' to the 'fun' Roger has made. Al laughs, a response which supports the conversational appropriateness of Roger's utterance and provides the local, locally historicized grounds for Roger to continue 'joking' by making puns of Ken's and his own remarks.

```
19 KEN And there's so ⌈many
20 ROGER            ⌊An' she threw a house war ⌈ming! hh!
21 KEN                                        ⌊Waita minute
22 (  ) ((cough))
23 AL heh heh
24 KEN Waita minute
25 ROGER hh a⌈bomb! hehh hh hehh hh
```

Again in line 25, Roger uses Al's laughter (line 23) as support for his taking the conversational next-turn, ignoring Ken's 'requests' for it in lines 21 and 24.

If, on the other hand, we examine Ken's utterances, we see that Ken is attempting to tell the part of his story that he is attempting to tell. Asking a question can be used as a mechanism for establishing the right to the next-turn-but-one.[4] Someone's 'answer' to it returns the next turn to the questioner. By giving a questioning intonation to his utterance in lines 15 and 16:

```
15 KEN⌊Well – ⌈the lady up the street just–just had one put in? About
17 AL         ⌊hehh hh hh hhh! ha
16 KEN four days ago?
18 (DAN) Mm hm?
```

Ken attempts to make his utterance into a question, therein seeking to elicit an appropriate response. Dan's 'mm hm?' provides the grounds for Ken to establish the motives for his asking the 'question' in the first place and, therein, continuing to speak. Ken is asking a question only in the sense that he wants a continuance marker – which he gets from Dan – to continue with the next turn.

Ken has already done the same thing in line 10, using a question to introduce his topically relevant material. He, in fact, has seen a fallout shelter and wants to tell about it.

```
10 KEN Have you seen some a' these – fallout shelters?
11 ROGER Yeah, I've seen so::me,
12 (1.0)
13 ROGER Be a ⌈nasty place tuh hide fro(h)m the ⌈co(h)ps
14,15 KEN   ⌊The lady –                        ⌊Well – ⌈the lady up the
street
```

Roger complies in line 11, but his possibly heard and witnessed pause, indicated by the comma, suggests that he has more to say, and Ken is slow to begin his turn (line 12). Roger turns Ken's question into the occasion for his own 'observation.' Ken does begin his turn in line 14, but it is now overlapping with Roger's utterance, to which he accedes. Ken then introduces the same organizational device, adding more background detail to the story he is working to tell.

13 ROGER Be a ⌈*nasty* place tuh hide fro(h)m the ⌈co(h)ps
14,15 KEN   ⌊The lady –   ⌊Well –
    KEN ⌈the lady up the street just–just had one put in? About
17 AL   ⌊hehh hh hh hhh! ha
16 KEN four days ago?

It appears from the transcript that Roger is working toward introducing these 'jokes' on fallout shelters, that Ken's utterances have become the occasion for his punning, and that Ken is trying, within that competing structuring of turns, for his turn to tell his 'serious' story. Against the background of Roger's jokes and Al's laughter, Ken will later insist on the seriousness of what he has to say – 'she's gotta *gun* in it' – although Ken's story has an ironic element of its own.

23 AL heh heh
24 KEN Waita minute
25 ROGER hh a ⌈*bomb*! hehh hh hehh hh
26 KEN   ⌊She's gotta *gun* in it.
27 KEN She's gotta gun hangin' there? And I said what's the gun for she said
28 in case any a' my *neigh*bors wann come in. ⌈Yuh know?

This competition gives Roger's utterances the character, for Ken, of a subterfuge of subconversational organization.

Although we have examined the transcript past the prospective 'post-overlap hitch,' we have *begun* to see how Ken is in competition with Al in line 17 for the conversational turn-at-talk.

13 ROGER Be a ⌈*nasty* place tuh hide fro(h)m the ⌈co(h)ps
14,15 KEN   ⌊The lady –   ⌊Well –
    KEN ⌈the lady up the street just–just had one put in? About
17 AL   ⌊hehh hh hh hhh! ha

Roger's later punning depends on this dual organization of the conversation – 'an' *she* threw a house warming' [italics added], 'a *bomb*.' It is not only a dual organization, but a dependent one – Roger uses the local historicity of his own remarks, Al's complicity, and the fact that Ken continues to introduce further talk on fallout shelters. In this way, in line 15, Ken is actually competing, during his continuing overlap with Al, with Roger and Al together for the next turn, making that overlap into an instance of overlapping turn competition. Al's laughter is not coincidental to the conversation; it is an integral part of the conversation's turn-organization. Thus, Ken's 'just–just' immediately following his overlap with Al's competing laughter appears to be tied to the ongoing, produced organization of turns and, hence, an instance of a 'post-overlap hitch.' We will shortly see how Ken's utterances in line 14 and 15 – 'the lady –,' 'well –' – already provides, and are used by Ken as the grounds for claiming his right to the turn for which Al's laughter is in competition.

As Shegloff has pointed out, there are conversationists who do not produce the overlap hitch. Moreover, they do not raise their volume of speech within the competing structure of an overlap. An overlap can continue for a long time, and co-conversationists that do this generally win the overlap hands down. By consistently denying the competing turn organization by speaking as if there were no overlap at all, they exhibit and retrospectively insist on the proper order of turns that they are exhibiting.

What the 'post-overlap hitch' means in terms of a cohort's order-productive work – whether, for example, it is simply a documented residue of co-conversationists' work or it is a re-gearing of a continuing utterance to a different conversational and organizational background – is an open question. I favor the second interpretation. The speaker who produces the 'hitch' recognizes that she has the entire possession of the turn, and this momentarily distracts her. The condition of the competing overlap is the absence of hearable pauses; this is the thing that the speaker who 'wins' the turn does not want to do. She repeats herself, and therein finds the things that she is continuing to say.

Before leaving the discussion of this transcript, we can also use it to illustrate co-conversationists' organizational work formatting turns-at-talk. Co-conversationists continually work to establish an order of speakers. Metaphorically, they line themselves up for the coming turns. They work to get the turn and, by doing so, can be heard to be speaking in turns. That the turn structure they are producing and exhibiting is heard by co-conversationists as a proper and constraining order underlies their accountable descriptions of 'overlaps' and 'interruptions' as such.

As an example, Ken's 'recycled turn' beginning – 'the lady' – in line 15 first appears as an overlap (line 14) with Roger's utterance.

```
13 ROGER  Be a ⌈nasty place tuh hide fro(h)m the ⌈co(h)ps
14,15 KEN      ⌊The lady –                        ⌊Well –
      KEN  ⌈the lady up the street just–just had one put in? About
17 AL      ⌊hehh hh hh hhh! ha
```

The first 'the lady' is an attempt to take the turn and indicates as well Ken's intention to do so. The heard, stretched pause of his 'well –' is Ken's gearing up for the end of Roger's utterance. Ken hears a possible turn completion point for Roger's turn coming up and 'positions' himself to be the next speaker. The recycled beginning, 'the lady', establishes the continuity of the utterance he has been working to introduce. This is Ken's local work – starting as early as line 3 ('hh') but clearly in line 10 ('have you seen some a' these – fallout shelters?') – in formatting the organization of turns to exhibit the appropriateness of his speaking next about 'the lady up the street.' Al's laughter in line 17, by exhibiting his appreciation and, therein, the appropriateness of Roger's comments, exhibits as well the propriety of Roger's continuing to insist on turns to make his puns. This is what makes up

Ken's, Al's, and Roger's competition for the turn in which Ken later produces a 'post-overlap hitch.'

Ken's attention to this work of formatting turns provides for the conversational irrelevance, to him, of Roger's jokes and the distracting devaluation of his remarks that they exhibit. By giving a questioning intonation to his utterances in lines 15 and 16, Ken is working for the 'mm hm?' in line 18 that establishes the next utterance as his to tell his story.

```
15 KEN   Well – ⌈the lady up the street just–just had one put in? About
17 AL            ⌊hehh hh hh hhh! ha
16 KEN   four days ago?
18 (DAN) Mm hm?
19 KEN   And there's so ⌈many –
```

As we have seen, this does not work. From the transcript, Dan is not dynamically involved in the conversation; his utterance appears as something of an aside – possibly a turn-organization-specific suggestion, at counter-purposes to Roger's and Al's efforts. Roger's punning and Al's appropriate next laughter generate and exhibit an organization of turns that undermines Ken's formatting efforts. At this point, Ken calls attention to, and simultaneously demands, his right to the turn: he tells Roger and Al to stop, not once but twice. In fact, he tells them precisely what he wants them to do – wait – so that he can have a turn to tell his story.

```
KEN   And there's so ⌈many
ROGER            ⌊An' she threw a house war ⌈ming! hh!
KEN                                          ⌊Waita minute
AL    heh heh
KEN   Waita minute
ROGER hh a ⌈bomb! hehh hh hehh hh
```

Even this does not work. Ken's insistence on the pointed thing of interest – that she had a *gun* – finally gives him the conversational 'space' to go on with his story.

```
ROGER hh a ⌈bomb! hehh hh hehh hh
KEN        ⌊She's gotta gun in it.
KEN   She's gotta gun hangin' there? And I said what's the gun for she said in
case any a' my neighbors wanna come in. ⌈Yuh know?
```

His questioning intonation – 'she's gotta gun hangin' there?' – dramatically emphasizes and makes problematic the substantive thing Ken has just claimed – that 'she's gotta *gun* in it' – indicating that he has more to say and that his next utterance will give the explanation. He is using his current utterance and intonation to preserve his current turn-at-talk. At long last, Ken has arranged for and taken the conversational time he needed to tell his story.

KEN: She's gotta gun hangin' there? And I said what's the gun for she said in case any a' my *neigh*bors wanna come in. ⌈Yuh know?

By rereading the entire transcript in terms of the co-conversationists' work at formatting turns – noting the overlaps, the pauses, the beginning attempts, and the different conversational themes – or simply by listening and attending to the lived-work of conversations – one sees that to say that co-conversationists take turns at talk, and to give disengaged, 'objective' rules for turn-taking, misses all the co-conversationists' work exhibiting and insuring that this is accountably so.

Chapter 12
'The baby cried'

For ethnomethodologists, conversational analysis is a jewel in the ethno-methodological crown. Ethnomethodologists and conversational analysts both agree that conversational analysis is serious research of the first order. Ethnomethodologists, however, interpret and re-examine conversation-analytic studies in ways that conversational analysts do not always approve. This and the following chapter give a working ethnomethodologist's introduction to conversational analysis. The historical remarks that I make are also a working person's history, something like the 'physicist's history of physics' that Feynman mentions in *QED: The Strange Theory of Light and Matter*.[1] My historical comments may not reflect a 'true' history of ethnomethodology; they are one practitioner's understanding of the development of some aspects of the field.

What might be called the 'first sequence' of conversational analysis is a story reportedly told by a child under three years of age.[2]

> The baby cried. The mommy picked it up.

To understand the importance of this story, some background material is necessary.

In the philosophical analysis of language, indexical expressions are expressions that depend on the circumstances of their utterance to gain a definiteness of sense and reference. They have also been referred to as 'token reflexives' and 'shifters.' The most accessible examples are words like 'he,' 'she,' 'it,' 'here,' 'there' and 'now.' Because of their dependence on situation and context, these expressions created problems for philosophers of language. The philosophers' aim was to build a formal logistic system as a model for language and explain the properties of language through the properties of that formal system. In the way that things sometimes get turned around, 'natural language' – as philosophers came to refer to an idealization of conversational speech – became a 'model' or imperfect realization of their logistic systems. Nevertheless, and because of this, there were immense practical problems involved in explaining indexical expressions both within logistic analysis and in the later studies of its theorized counterpart, 'natural language.'

When Garfinkel began to examine the ways in which a description or account is part of the setting in which it occurs, he saw conversationists' use of indexicals as a 'perspicuous phenomenon' that could be used to investigate that relationship. Co-conversationists' embodied presence to each other – the distance between them, the intonation and voicing they give to an utterance, their directed looks, the local historicity of their actions and of things just said, their gestures and facial expressions – gives their utterances their definiteness of meaning, or lack thereof, for co-conversationists. Since indexical expressions depend so heavily on this witnessed but unarticulated work of speaking definitely, the examination of their use promised material access to the order-productive lived-work of speaking meaningfully.

As it turned out, indexical expressions began to become an all-inclusive category. It includes, for example, the use of verb tense. If a baby is not crying and someone says 'The baby cried,' the utterance is heard as a reference to an event in the past that other co-conversationists might not have been present to hear. If the baby is currently crying, 'The baby cried' could be a reference to a past occurrence, or it could be hearably incorrect usage. Nouns themselves are indexical expressions. The definiteness of reference for co-conversationists of 'the baby' and 'the mommy' is a feature of their ongoing activities. Even the lack of a specific reference – an absent particularity of the mommy and the baby – is a situated feature of an utterance – in the case of the 'first sequence,' possibly allowing it to be heard as a story 'proper.' No matter what precision or care someone gives to her speech, minimally that precision and the need for it are tied to the circumstances of the utterance. In this way, the term 'indexical expressions' can be seen to apply to all conversational utterances.

Garfinkel was not actually interested in the real or underlying structure of language or speech such that these expressions gain their definiteness of reference. He was interested in the missed 'ordinariness' of speech. The lived, embodied work of a conversation makes the definiteness of reference of an indexical expression the most ordinary of occurrences. The ordinariness of a conversation does not create problems for co-conversationists; philosophers and linguists had previously paid no attention to it. Yet, that ordinariness is an essential part of conversational behavior. Co-conversationists use and depend on it to produce and manage their conversations; linguists and philosophers depend on it to find examples for their analyses. The ordinariness of an utterance was the phenomenon ethnomethodologists were most interested in, and Garfinkel used a number of devices – such as having students wear inverting lenses or having them wear the glasses and carry the canes of the blind – to disrupt it and, therein, to exhibit the work that was required to make it that way. By initially focusing on indexical expressions, Garfinkel sought to rediscover the ordinariness of speech as itself a produced feature of a conversation, an accomplishment of the lived-work of ordinary speech.

Although only a small part of the late Harvey Sacks's studies, his analysis of the 'first sequence':

The baby cried. The mommy picked it up.

came to represent the opening of an entirely new domain for ethno-methodological research.

Sacks began his analysis of the 'first sequence' by pointing out that when a co-conversationist hears this story, she hears that the 'mommy' is the mommy of the 'baby' and that the 'it' that the mommy picked up is her baby. *Prima facie*, there is nothing in the sequence of utterances that makes this true. That is just the way that it is heard. What Sacks meant by 'heard' was that the sequence is heard in its definiteness, not that it could not be heard differently. Nothing critical depended on his analysis being absolutely correct in this one instance. The phenomenon that he had begun to elucidate is that the analyze-ability, or story-ability, or hear-ability, or objectivity of the sequence is part of the sequence itself. The 'mommy' is the mommy of the 'baby,' and she picked her baby up. That analyzability is part of the way the story was told and heard.

For some of Sacks's collaborators, this notion of hearability came to be something else. Conversational analysis became its own discipline with its own professional work practices, and these were used to justify the practical adequacy of conversational-analytic findings. Like the ethnomethodologists, conversational analysts were beleaguered by the criticism, slighting treatment, and, often, the disrespect of professional sociologists. Absolutely right in insisting that the grounds for the analysis of their conversational materials should be what was hearable on their tape recordings, some conversational analysts came to insist, and interrupt, and verbally 'man-handle' anyone who offered a different 'hearing' or organizationally different interpretation of an utterance. They used the notion of what a 'member,' i.e. a co-conversationist in a conversation's local production cohort, definitely hears as a means of justifying their work practices. Their notion of a 'member' became a straightforward analytic device that they enforced as the grounds for collaborative discussion and research.

In terms of indexical expressions, the amazing thing that Sacks did in his analysis of the 'first sequence' was to make available a massive domain of interactional phenomena that fills speech and the hearing of it. He had discovered the 'missing interaction' of conversation. Indexical expressions gain their definiteness of reference through the ways that co-conversationists speak, and they speak in such a way so as to be heard saying the things that they say. How do they accomplish this?

What Sacks did next was brilliant in all of its details, but, as I think Sacks himself later found, wrong. His use of tape-recorded conversations and transcripts distanced him from the witnessed, lived-work of co-conversationists' production of an ordinary conversation. The gestures, the pointing, the embodied presence, the local historicity of things said, the previous definiteness of an utterance, the actions of co-conversationists and the activities in which they were engaged were not, and could not be, part of the examined transcripts and tape recordings. Later conversational analysts would try to provide for the presence of these aspects of conversations as things coincidental to the conversational structures they documented, as dual and reinforcing actions rather than as an integral part of a conversation.

What Sacks did was to build a model in order to explain how conversationists speak in the accountable, hearable ways that they do. He is often quoted as saying that he wanted to build a 'machine' that would provide for the details of conversational behavior. He began to construct member-(i.e. co-conversationist-)relevant category devices and rules for their use. For example, in the story:

The baby cried. The mommy picked it up.

he claimed that when a co-conversationist hears 'mommy,' she hears in the word 'mommy' the relevance of the 'family' as the category of expressions that both 'baby' and 'mommy' belong to.

Whether or not I get the exact use of the member-relevant category rules correct, the reader will understand their general explanatory use. The 'family' is an *adequate* category for co-conversationists to use in that it includes both the 'baby' and the 'mommy,' and it is the smallest possible relevant category, as opposed, for example, to babies and adults. In this way, it is *economic*, as is the hearing of the 'it' as being the baby, the 'it' belonging to the same category, the 'family.' Not only is the use of 'baby' and 'mommy' *consistent* with the member-relevant category, so is the 'it.' When a baby cries, so the argument went, one of the categorically 'proper' things a mommy can do is pick it up to calm it.

All these things were not only supposed to be the practical reasoning the hearer of the story was engaged in; they were supposed to be the practical reasoning of the speaker in producing the utterances so that they would be heard in that way. 'Practical reasoning' referred to a co-conversationist's producing an utterance so that it would be heard in the accountable way that it was, not to a reflective activity. The analyzability of the 'first sequence' is part of that sequence itself. However, as the category devices and rules began to be developed, the 'machine' being built seemed increasingly similar to linguists' theorized constructions. The utterances, and the lived-work of conversation surrounding and embedded in them that they themselves are, were no longer self-sufficient – as they are for co-conversationists – to win the day.

As this first direction of conversation studies developed, the world started to get full of categories and rules for their use. Many of them were simply the attempts of conversational analysts to explain the difficulties of analyzing the utterances that occasioned their introduction. Though not an oppressive feature of Sacks's work, 'rule-governed behavior' became the underlying principle that allowed some conversational analysts, in the studies that later developed, to insist that the co-conversationists on a tape recording were speaking the way that the analysts said they were. For ethnomethodologists, it was clear from their studies that practical action is not done according to rule, but Garfinkel began to examine what 'following a rule' is as a practical method. He studied, for example, how people play chess so that their actions exhibit that they are following the rules-of-the-game. And he studied how people play chess while wearing inverting lenses to find the problems that they have, therein exhibiting the work of playing the game that is essential to its conduct but otherwise found uninteresting.

On one hand, Sacks's discovery of 'the missing organizational what' of conversation opened a new aspect of the ordinariness of conversation for investigation. On the other, it put the earlier ethnomethodological interests concerning co-conversationists' embodied presence to each other in the background. This is one of the continuing differences between the ethnomethodological use of conversation-analytic materials and that of conversational analysts. But more pointedly, some conversational analysts came to insist that the structures of conversation they had found were 'objective' structures. They turned away from the examination of the produced ordinariness and objectivity of practical action as an organizational phenomenon. The examination of conversational behavior and of conversational analysts' own materials points to a much greater richness of their findings than they want to allow.

Sacks, either out of dissatisfaction or because of more abiding interests, eventually stopped his work on member-relevant category devices. The category devices and the rules for their use – the original Sacksian machinery of conversation – had become another formal structure, similar to those of the linguists and natural language philosophers. In contrast, however, the phenomena that Sacks had tried to explain – the tape-recorded conversations – were not idealized models whose relevance and adequacy were ensured by the work practices of a professional academic discipline. Sacks had stayed close to the actual phenomena of lived conversation. By subduing the stress on rules and categories, the Sacksian *corpus* is a wonderful collection illuminating the detailed work co-conversationists do to speak and hear co-conversationists speaking about just the things they are speaking about. That the 'mommy' was the mommy of the 'baby,' that the 'it' was the 'baby,' and that 'picking it up' was the response to the baby's crying are all part of the work of producing and managing conversational activities. All these things are 'in the words,' but they are 'in there' because that is part of the work of practically accountable ordinary speech.

Chapter 13
The lived-orderliness of conversation

In the midst of his studies of member-relevant category devices, Sacks made a discovery of something so ordinary that its ordinariness almost overwhelms its momentousness. It was already implicit in his analysis of the 'first sequence':

> The baby cried. The mommy picked it up.

In addition to the 'mommy' being the mommy of the 'baby' and the 'baby' being the 'it' that she picked up, Sacks pointed out that the utterances were produced and heard in a temporal order. The first 'utterance' was 'The baby cried.' The second was 'The mommy picked it up.' For co-conversationists this temporal ordering is a consequential one. The order in which the utterances of the 'first sequence' are said is tied to the temporal order in which the events the sequence reports are heard to have occurred. First the baby cried, then the mommy picked it up. And the mommy is heard to have picked the baby up because it was crying.

The reader might want to contrast the 'first sequence' to a possible alternative:

> The mommy picked it up. The baby cried.

Sacks's point was that the ordering of utterances was something co-conversationists do to be heard properly. Co-conversationists use and rely on the practical skills of speaking and listening – including the interior, temporal building of an utterance or sequence – to speak meaningfully with each other. As written sentences, the story the 'first sequence' told could possibly be seen not to be in the words, but in the hearing of them. For co-conversationists, however, it is heard in the words; it is the practically accountable thing being said. Co-conversationists' practical actions and practical reasoning are what both the sequence and the sense of that sequence consist of; the way co-conversationists speak is identical to the way they make their speech 'accountable'. Yet this interactional phenomenon was missing in all previous accounts of linguistic behavior.

For Sacks, there was something deeper in the 'first sequence.' It is a 'story.' That is how it is heard, and that was how it was described. But that it is a story seems to depend on the fact that it was told in two 'units.' 'The baby cried' was the first unit; 'The mommy picked it up' was the second. If a co-conversationist would ever say 'When the baby cried, the mommy picked it up,' this would not be heard in quite the same way. It could be praise, an explanation, a complaint, a causal account, a description, but not quite a 'story.' The story-ableness of the story as a story – its practically accountable character as a story – is tied in some way to the fact that its telling was done as a pair of utterances.

Later, Sacks and his collaborators spent considerable time developing the notion of 'adjacency pair' structures such as questions and answers, and summons and responses. It was another discovery that was turned into a formal structure. Co-conversationists were supposed to use and rely on that pair structure to make their utterances into what they were, as if a questioner needed to hear the response in order to know that she had asked a question. Originally, however, Sacks's observation was simply that for the 'first sequence's' story to be told, there had to be more than one 'utterance.' Therein, a co-conversationist had to arrange for the conversational time in which she could take two 'turn units.'

Let us return to a portion of the transcript used in Chapter 11.

```
KEN ⌊Well – ⌈the lady up the street just–just had one put in? About
AL          ⌊hehh hh hh hhh! ha
KEN four days ago?
(DAN) Mm hm?
KEN And there's so ⌈many
ROGER              ⌊An' she threw a house war ⌈ming! hh!
KEN                                           ⌊Waita minute
(  ) ((cough))
AL heh heh
KEN Waita minute
ROGER hh a ⌈bomb! hehh hh hehh hh
KEN         ⌊She's gotta gun in it.
KEN She's gotta gun hangin' there? And I said what's the gun for she said in
case any a' my neighbors wanna come in. ⌈Yuh know?
```

Ken has had to work for a turn to tell about the 'gun hangin' there.' But that is not really the point of Ken's conversational work, the point of the story Ken is trying to tell. The 'gun' that is introduced in one utterance is also a device for explaining the import of its being there in the next utterance – if the so-called neighbors try to come in, the lady intends to shoot them. Ken is explaining what the import of the gun is. That he is depends on his introduction of the thing to be explained, and to do so it took two 'turn units.' Arranging for those 'turn units' was the lived conversational work Ken was engaged in, and taking them was his accomplishment.

The discovery Sacks made was that if co-conversationists are providing the conversational 'space,' i.e. time, to have two of some type of units, they are providing that space in *something*. The discovery was that co-conversationists are having a conversation. That is the object that they, as a production cohort, are producing and managing.

In some ways this discovery was one more step removed from the understanding of the local production of meaningful speech. It was also a tremendous advance. Much of what co-conversationists do and say – like asking a question, pausing, interrupting, agreeing, laughing, repeating – has an organizational referent. They are the things conversationists do to 'get the conversation done.' It was this discovery – the discovery of the naturally organized conversation – with which Sacks and his collaborators began the investigation of a conversation's production cohort's order-productive work of producing and managing a conversation. They studied, and his collaborators continue to study, the work of a conversational opening, the organizational import of asking a question, how co-conversationists open up and provide for conversational endings, how they actually end a conversation, how they use conversational 'structures' to say the things that they want to say like complaints or explanations or stories, how those things are what they accountably are because of their organizational structure, and how what co-conversationists say and want to say are tied to the organization of a conversation itself. A local production cohort organizes a conversation, and they do so naturally as part of what they are doing. In many ways, that is just what they are doing. This was Sacks's discovery, the discovery of conversation as a naturally organized activity.

To bring to a close this introduction to conversational analysis, one more of Sacks's seminal discoveries should be told. Again, the ordinariness of the original observation both is and belies its fundamental significance. Although its observation was already implicitly present in conversation-analytic studies, its articulation revolutionized the field and had a profound effect on all of ethnomethodology. In order to appreciate it, it is necessary to understand that Sacks had not only 'discovered' conversations as naturally organized activities, he had discovered them as 'social facts' or 'organizational objects.'

Borrowing from Durkheim, Garfinkel had developed the notion of the 'social object,' the 'social fact,' or the 'organizational object.' What Garfinkel did was to analyze, not the notion of a social object, but what a social object is that makes it just that. The analysis is straight Garfinkel, something like straight whiskey, and I take the following principally from my notes of his lectures. While reading this analysis, it is profitable to keep in mind conversations and formatted queues as examples. In the former, the produced turn-taking organization is their identifying feature; greetings or openings, questions, stories, complaints and closings are among their 'organizational events.' In the latter, a formatted queue's exhibited order of service – one's place in line, the queue's direction, the end of the line – is its identifying feature, and taking one's place in line, moving appropriately forward and maintaining position, filling open service bays, exhibiting impatience, interrogative posturing, and 'line talk' are among its organizational events.

The first thing Garfinkel pointed out was that a social object is not an abstract entity; it is not something that someone has to interpret in order to see that it is what it is. It is observed or witnessed. It seems as if it is already there and always has been there; its presence is such that it *is* already and always there. It is a familiar thing, part of the natural world. And it is hopelessly sensible. The social object is made up of its material, witnessable, and witnessed details. It is not an anonymous setting, but a personalized one, made up of the witnessable and witnessed particulars of its production cohort's actions. Moreover, these objects are analyzable or accountable or story-able. That they can be named is part of their analyzability. So is the fact that the actions of its local production cohort are seen and described in the ways that they are. That analyzability does not depend on professional training; it is available to vulgar competence. Social objects are not hidden objects, but recognized, ordinary, commonplace. And they have a massive presence. When someone comes to inquire about them, there is a retrospective illusion that they offer themselves as the cause and the source for the inquiry; they offer themselves as being independent of every method of finding them or talking about them. Therein, they have a transcendental character. They also have a transcendental presence. The social object seems to stand above, or to be greater than, the actions of its production cohort. It is an 'object,' the recognized thing that the local cohort is producing. And that object is a moral object through and through; it is right and proper that the object – the formatted queue, for example – is the way that it is. It is a moral fact of life, and the actions of its local production cohort are moral or immoral actions, like butting-in-line or ignoring a question and speaking out of turn. The actions of a social object's production cohort are constrained by the object that that cohort is itself accountably producing.

To illustrate the problem of social order, Garfinkel would often use the example of the formatted queue. Before its local production cohort – 'the people in the line' – have organized themselves into a queue, there is no queue, and the queue has no properties. In coming together, by positioning themselves and doing all the this-particular-queue-specific relevant work of exhibiting and maintaining that queue's particular witnessed orderlinesses, a queue takes on all of its accountable properties – who is behind whom, where the end is, who is first in line, what the direction of the queue is, who is in, who is out, and who are together. All of a queue's properties are locally produced, yet a queue is seen by its production cohort as a pre-existing, propertied object. The formatted queue is a 'social' or 'organizational object.' This is the amazing, mundane, uncelebrated achievement of its local production cohort. Queue members can be seen to stand in their places, impatiently wiggling, as if and in fact trapped by the constraints and 'morality' of a queue's witnessed structures.

For ethnomethodologists, the problem of social order is the problem of investigating – through real-worldly, materially motivated studies – how a production cohort does 'that' and what 'that' is. What does a social object consist of, for its production cohort, as practical action and reasoning? How is the 'social object' – and, therein, its accountable properties and its accountability as a social object itself – produced, managed, preserved and changed? These questions concern the very particularity, and witnessed particularity, of a production cohort's organizational work. The local cohort ignores the work of the production of the object, but, at the same time, they witness and use it. The woman who butts in line is a 'jerk' in and as the way she does the butting. The person who goes to the end of the line, positions herself, and constrains her movements witnessably preserves the witnessable orderlinesses of that specific queue. To see to the front of the line, a queue member will take a partial step to the left, put her weight on her left foot but 'anchor' the right one, bending and stretching her body to peer ahead as if forced to move and look in that way, but doing so to exhibit her rightful place and the purposefulness of her actions. The social object has a transcendental presence, but it is seen to have that presence, by its local production cohort, in and as the produced features of the object itself. The production cohort does what it does to maintain and preserve that exhibited presence, and that makes up its transcendental presence as well. The queue member sees the formatted character of the queue in and as the way this-specific-queue's production cohort have positioned and distanced themselves. She finds the end of the queue, the gap through which to pass, or the person in front of whom to butt in and as the witnessed particularities of just that queue.

Prior to Sacks's 'discovery' of conversations, he and his collaborators had studied the organizational work (if not the lived-organizational work) of a conversation's ordinary events – like questions, greetings, complaints, explanations, stories, formulations, salutations. The realization that a conversation is a social object, like a formatted queue, was simultaneously the recognition that co-conversationists do greetings as openings (and, sometimes, as openings and endings), that they open up closings or make time to tell a story or voice a complaint, all as part of, and the intimate details of, producing and managing the social object. The local historicity of what they are doing, as part of the conversation, occasions their own formulations of what they are talking about or of how they came to be talking about it. That they are doing these things and that they are constrained to do them in the ways that they are – that they are opening a topic for discussion or beginning to close down the conversation, that someone is interrupting or has appropriately spoken next – are, for the production cohort itself, the recognized orderlinesses of the conversation. A conversation is a social object.

It is in this domain – the investigation of the 'social object' as a produced object – that perhaps Sacks's greatest discovery takes on its significance. To see this, let us return one last time to the following section of a transcript.

KEN ⌊Well – ⌈the lady up the street just–just had one put in? About
AL ⌊hehh hh hh hhh! ha
KEN four days ago?
(DAN) Mm hm?

Are Ken's utterances questions? He gives them, or their endings, a questioning intonation and apparently gets, from Dan, a continuing device, an 'Mm hm?' telling him to go on. But is the questioning intonation of Dan's 'Mm hm' part of that continuance – asking for more – or is it a questioning of Ken's intonation and, therein, a continuance device? On the surface, Ken's utterances do not look like questions at all. Are they? Without the actual tape recordings, or without being present to hear and observe the conversation, or perhaps not even then, it may be impossible to say more. It is in this context that Sacks's discovery is exhibited.

Sacks's discovery was that a conversation is done in turns – that the identifying orderlinesses of a conversation depend on its produced turn-taking organization. A co-conversationist can do the intonational work of asking a question, but the specificity of what the utterance is doing particularly – its fine shading of reference – is a reference as well to the turn-taking organization. Co-conversationists can name an utterance as a 'question,' or they can ask 'Are you asking me?' This is part of the produced analyzability of the orderliness of co-conversationists' lived-work. But it is not quite right to say that a conversationist asked a 'question' or, as another instance, that she 'interrupted.' Sometimes conversational analysts use the notion of a 'member' or a 'member's hearing' to insist on the naive or natural naming of an action or sequence of actions. This is the natural perspective, but it is the natural perspective of a co-conversationist as a practical analyst of practical action. That a co-conversationist might call an utterance a 'question' is not because that is all she sees and hears, but because of what she sees and hears. In the same way, a queue member might say that someone was 'butting,' but that butting is seen in the specific particulars that made it that. A local cohort's formulations – a 'question,' an 'interruption,' someone 'butting' – are themselves part of the naturally organized ordinary activity they are engaged in producing. They are part of the produced analyzability of that 'event.'

The import of Sacks's discovery of the turn-taking organization was that it was not quite right to say that a co-conversationist asked a 'question.' Co-conversationists do what they do to get what they want or to get what they get. It is part of the work of the conversation. They do not hear a 'question'; they hear the particular thing, or mis-hear the particular thing as some other particular thing – organizationally and substantively, substantively organizational and organizationally substantive – that the co-conversationist's utterance is doing. A conversation's produced turn-taking organization is the orderliness of co-conversationists' lived-work of producing and managing the social object – the conversation – that lets co-conversationists do the conversational things that they do. It is the produced, witnessed, identifying orderliness of a conversation as a conversation.

The 'discovery' and examination of turn-organization radicalized all conversation-analytic structures and revolutionized the field. It supplied technical access to the detailed, particularistic, lived-work of the witnessed orderlinesses of co-conversationists' work, for and by co-conversationists, of producing the social object – a conversation. From the naive standpoint – and from the derivative perspective of the disengaged analyst – conversationists are 'questioning' and 'complaining,' 'explaining' and 'telling stories,' 'formulating' and 'conjecturing,' 'beginning' and 'ending.' But all this is accomplished through, and recognized as being accomplished through, a conversation's turn-taking organization; the analyzability of what co-conversationists are doing as 'questioning' or 'explaining,' for the production cohort, is part and parcel of a conversation's locally produced and managed turn-taking organization as well. Co-conversationists use that organization to do, and as the occasion to do, all the particular things they are doing – like 'questioning' and 'complaining,' 'explaining' and 'telling stories,' 'formulating' and 'conjecturing,' 'beginning' and 'ending.' The end of a conversation is a local cohort's arrangement of the end of the turns-at-talk. Sacks's discovery of the turn-taking organization provided the analyzable orderliness of a conversation's production cohort's actions and, therein, it provided for the local cohort's recognition of the situated, transcendental presence of the 'social object.' It helped radicalize the notion of a 'social fact' itself, locating its presence in and as the witnessable orderlinesses of co-conversationists' situated, conversation-specific, substantively specific, order-productive, ordinary, organizational, conversational work.

The 'received' version of Sacks's discovery is that the turn-taking organization is an 'objective' structure that co-conversationists use. All the insisting in the world does not make this so. We have seen in this *Guide* that the formatting of turns-at-talk is part of a local production cohort's work and accomplishment. Co-conversationists use the orderlinesses or 'structures' of the conversation that they are locally building, and the local historicity of those orderlinesses and the work of their construction, as the witnessable, tactile, accountable grounds for producing and using those same structures. They do it all locally, *in situ*, with the devices – their mouths, their eyes, their bodies – that they have on hand. This is their amazing, tremendous, ordinary, and ignored achievement.

Chapter 14
A mathematical proof

In the chapters that follow, this *Guide* offers an introduction to the ethnomethodology of mathematics. For some, any mathematics is already too much. I hope such readers will find these chapters profitable. Chapter 20 helps place them within a larger perspective. In order to make the material more accessible, the theorems that will be considered have been taken from elementary geometry. The detailed examination of mathematicians' work inevitably leads to all the technicalities of real-world mathematics – on the one hand troublesome for the uninitiated, on the other refreshing when compared with the romance and trivializations found, for example, in the sociology of science. No trivializations will be involved in our treatment. The proofs of the theorems we will consider are no less mathematics, and the lived-work of those proofs no less identifying of mathematical practice, than the most sophisticated proofs of contemporary mathematics.

The re-examination of conversational turn-taking given in the preceding chapter is an example of the ethnomethodological radicalization of the problem of social order. It illustrates what ethnomethodologists understand by the problem of social order. Everywhere, the production of the orderlinesses of practical action is a recognizable accomplishment of and by a local production cohort. All the properties of the social order are produced and made visible locally, *in situ*. Everywhere, the social, moral, constraining order is a completely localized arena of practical action and reasoning.

The ethnomethodological investigation of mathematics gains its significance from within this 'perspective.' It is pointless to argue whether or not mathematical theorems are 'true.' In a sense, they are everything we know about disengaged truth. This is not because there is a disengaged, objective position from which to evaluate them; the history of mathematical logic teaches us the insuperable problems involved in mathematically establishing such a position. But while mathematicians acknowledge this lack of a precise global justification for their work practices, the practical rigor of those practices is an indisputable achievement.

The early Greeks were amazed, perplexed, and deeply concerned that reasoners could come together and, through their own situated actions – by drawing figures in the sand and reasoning about them – demonstrate that something was anonymously the case. Provers could show that a theorem of mathematics was 'true' for anyone, anywhere, anytime. Their proofs showed that some descriptive statement about the 'world' of idealized drawings and objects that their own hand-drawn figures made available was objectively true. This is the witnessed achievement of a local production cohort of provers – a mathematical theorem does not depend on the particulars of their situated actions. Yet, somehow, the disengaged adequacy of their work practices is the achievement of those selfsame, local and occasioned practices.

The aim of the next few chapters is to indicate how the adequacy (or rigor) of a mathematical proof is a situated, practical accomplishment and how that accomplishment is a 'problem,' for provers, in the local production of social order. In this chapter, I present the proof of a theorem of Euclidean geometry. The proof is given in an informal manner, similar to the way it would be presented in a blackboard demonstration. In order to do this, I have used the devices of repeated figures and bracketed indexicals like '[this]' for which the reader must examine the figures to find the definiteness of their reference. The next two chapters animate this proof through a discussion of its lived-work. For the moment, however, an actual proof must be given. The ethnomethodology of mathematics concerns the witnessable, material details, for a local cohort of provers, of their own work practices – that is, it concerns mathematical practice. For the ethnomethodologist, there is no alternative to this commitment to the real-worldly details of practical action and reasoning.

The theorem we will consider is that the measure of an inscribed angle is half the measure of its intercepted arc. If α is the inscribed angle depicted in Fig. 14.1, its intercepted arc is the darkened portion of the circle.

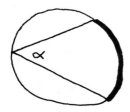

FIG. 14.1

In Fig. 14.2, C is the center of the circle. The measure of an arc of a circle

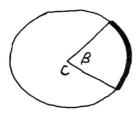

FIG. 14.2

is defined to be the measure $m(\beta)$ of the central angle β that that arc is said to subtend. Thus, as in Fig. 14.3, we wish to show that

$$m(\alpha) = 1/2m(\beta).$$

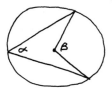

Fig. 14.3

To prove this theorem three separate cases must be distinguished. One case is where one of the sides of the inscribed angle [meets] the center of the circle (see Fig. 14.4(a)). Another is the case where the center of the circle is in the [interior] of the angle (Fig. 14.4(b)). The third is where the center of the circle lies in the part of the plane [exterior] to the angle (Fig. 14.4(c)). We must show that the theorem is true for each of these cases.

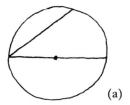 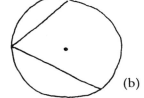 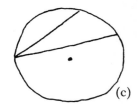

(a)　　　　(b)　　　　(c)

Fig. 14.4

Let us begin by considering the case where one of the sides of the angle contains the center of the circle. By drawing the central angle subtended by the intercepted arc (Fig. 14.5(a)) and labelling [the relevant angles] (Fig. 14.5(b)), we see that we must show that the measure of the inscribed angle α is half the measure of β.

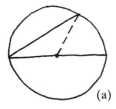 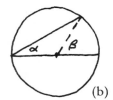

(a)　　　　(b)

Fig. 14.5

Notice first that [this line segment] marked with a crossing line (Fig. 14.6(a)) is a radius of the circle, as is [this line segment] marked similarly (Fig. 14.6(b)). This means that the two line segments have equal length and,

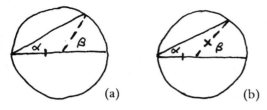

(a)   (b)

FIG. 14.6

therefore, that [this triangle] (Fig. 14.7) is an isosceles triangle. In an isosceles triangle, the base angles are congruent; they are marked accordingly

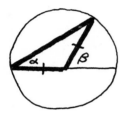

FIG. 14.7

in Fig. 14.8. Congruent angles must have equal measure – otherwise the notion of measure would be poorly defined. In fact, from a modern

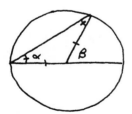

FIG. 14.8

perspective, 'congruent angles' are really the same angle. By labeling the angles accordingly, labelling the third angle of the triangle γ (Fig. 14.9) and noting that the sum of the measures of the angles of a triangle is 180°, we see that two times the measure of α plus the measure of γ equals 180° or

$$2m(\alpha) + m(\gamma) = 180°.$$

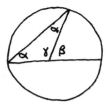

FIG. 14.9

Observing that angles β and γ together form a straight angle, we see that the measure of β plus the measure of γ equals 180° as well:

$$m(\beta) + m(\gamma) = 180°.$$

Since two angle αs and angle γ together are the same as angle β and angle γ together (see Fig. 14.9), two times α must equal β.

More formally, equating the two expressions given above – things equal to the same thing being equal – we obtain

$$2m(\alpha) + m(\gamma) = m(\beta) + m(\gamma).$$

Subtracting equals from equals gives

$$2m(\alpha) = m(\beta).$$

Thus, two times the measure of α equals the measure of β, and, hence

$$m(\alpha) = \tfrac{1}{2}\, m(\beta).$$

The theorem has been proved for the first case.

The proof of the theorem for the remaining cases uses one of the ever-popular tricks of mathematics. In the second case (see Fig. 14.10), by

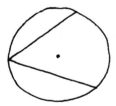

FIG. 14.10

drawing the subtended central angle (Fig. 14.11), introducing the diameter of the circle that passes through the vertex of the inscribed angle [thus] (Fig. 14.12) and labeling the angles as in Fig. 14.13, the second case reduces to the first one.

From our previous work we know that

$$m(\alpha) = \tfrac{1}{2}\, m(\beta).$$

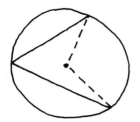

FIG. 14.11

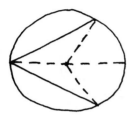

FIG. 14.12

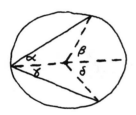

FIG. 14.13

and

$$m(\gamma) = \tfrac{1}{2}\, m(\delta).$$

In our present circumstances, like those of the early Greeks, we can see from the figure that, since

$$m(\alpha) = \tfrac{1}{2}\, m(\beta)$$

and

$$m(\gamma) = \tfrac{1}{2}\, m(\delta),$$

the measure of the inscribed angle $\alpha + \gamma$ equals half the measure of $\beta + \delta$, the measure of the intercepted arc:

$$m(\alpha + \gamma) = \tfrac{1}{2}\, m(\beta + \delta).$$

In contemporary mathematics, a more formal derivation is possible. A 'measure' is defined to have the property of 'finite additivity':

$$m(\alpha + \gamma) = m(\alpha) + m(\gamma) = \tfrac{1}{2}\,m(\beta) + \tfrac{1}{2}\,m(\delta) = \tfrac{1}{2}\,m(\beta + \delta).$$

Hence, the measure of the inscribed angle $\alpha + \gamma$ equals half the measure of the angle subtended by the intercepted arc $\beta + \delta$. By reducing the second case to the first one, we have proved the theorem for the case where an inscribed angle contains the center of the circle in its interior.

The case where the center of the circle is exterior to the inscribed angle is reduced to the first case in a similar manner, completing the proof of the theorem. In [the drawing] (Fig. 14.14(a)) we want to show that the measure of [this angle] (in Fig. 14.14(b)) is half the measure of [this one] (in Fig. 14.14(c)).

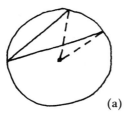 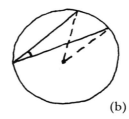 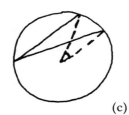

(a)   (b)   (c)

Fig. 14.14

Drawing the diameter of the circle through the vertex of the inscribed angle (Fig. 14.15) and labeling the figure [thus] (Fig. 14.16), we need to

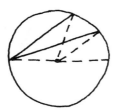

Fig. 14.15

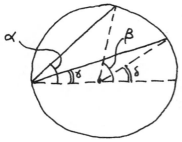

Fig. 14.16

show that the measure of α minus γ (α − γ being the inscribed angle) is half the measure of β minus δ (β − δ being the central angle subtended by the intercepted arc). By the first case

$$m(\alpha) = \tfrac{1}{2}\, m(\beta)$$

and

$$m(\gamma) = \tfrac{1}{2}\, m(\delta).$$

We see in the diagram that the measure of α minus γ therefore equals half the measure of β minus δ. Thus,

$$m(\alpha - \gamma) = \tfrac{1}{2}\, m(\beta - \delta)$$

and the proof is completed.

Chapter 15
The lived-work of proving: first observations

No less than the early Greeks, contemporary mathematicians are amazed by the phenomenal presence of proofs such as the one given in the preceding chapter. If a mathematician sees the concerns of the theorem as being peculiarly Euclidean, she is no less entranced by its witnessed achievement. The proof demonstrated that for any inscribed angle, positioned in a circle in any way, the measure of that angle is half the measure of its intercepted arc. No less than the very latest mathematical discovery, such a proof is 'elegant' and 'beautiful' – in its simplicity and immediacy, perhaps even more so. Each time a prover reacquaints herself with it, the proof is seen again as a discovery. The prover rediscovers the properties of Euclidean circles, angles, and triangles, and the reasoning of the proof, that makes the theorem true. She experiences that reasoning and the innovations of the proof as a pleasing, aesthetic demonstration of their discovery – the proof itself. Is there anything that ethnomethodology can contribute to an understanding of that proof? Wherein does its rigor and elegance lie?

For many years, ethnomethodologists have been engaged in studies of the professions – law, sociology, medicine, long-haul truck driving, experimental biochemistry. The emphasis of these studies is not on the professions as 'occupations' nor on practitioners' work practices as 'labor'; it continually is placed on real-world actions, on the detailed 'doings' of a profession's practitioners. Ethnomethodologists have attempted to gain access to what is identifying, for the working practitioner, in and as the details of her work, that make that work recognizably and uniquely the work of her profession. Always present in their investigations is the contrast between lived-work and its theorized renderings – between speech and language, between conversation and discourse, between lived-work and occupations or labor. What, for the local production cohort, makes it real, professionally competent surgery rather than the work of leeches? What makes it long-haul trucking instead of the family relocation in a rental truck? What makes lecturing in sociology different from lecturing in chemistry? What makes the work of the professions distinctively and witnessably that work?

When the ethnomethodology of mathematics was first undertaken, it was intended as an investigation of the 'foundations' of mathematics. 'Foundations,' however, was not understood in terms of a disengaged accounting procedure such as those of mathematical logic; instead, it was understood in terms of the situated work practices of professional mathematicians – that is, as the living foundations or 'genetic origins' of the discipline. The ethnomethodology of mathematics was the attempt to find the lived, identifying work of mathematical theorem proving. The investigation was directed toward discovering what the situated practices of proving are that make them the work of rigorous proving.

In order to develop this theme adequately, this chapter and the next describe some of the situated, lived-work of our proof concerning inscribed angles. Later, we will see that the written proof that was given was really only 'half' of the actual proof – it was a 'proof-account.' The other 'half' of the proof was its 'lived-work.' Such lived-work has a phenomenal presence throughout any proof. It is essential to a local cohort of provers' production and exhibition of a proof-account as a practically adequate, disengaged description of its associated proof. But, at the same time, this practical accomplishment of a proof's lived-work gives that lived-work its seen, yet shadowy, ephemeral and ignored presence. Our first task is to exhibit what some of that lived-work is.

To begin, let us consider a somewhat innocuous feature of the lived-work of our proof. Independently of the existence of a contemporary, rigorous definition of an angle, a drawn angle or the angle of a finished proof-figure, such as the one in Fig. 15.1, is *seen* in terms of the witnessed relationship

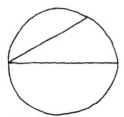

FIG. 15.1

between the 'sides' of the angle and the plane sector that those sides enclose (Fig. 15.2).

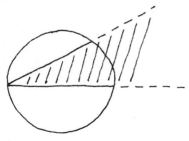

FIG. 15.2

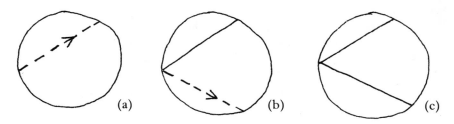

FIG. 15.3

The temporal drawing of an angle (Fig. 15.3) is seen in its demarcation of that plane sector. So is the manner in which an angle, like ∠ACB (Fig. 15.4),

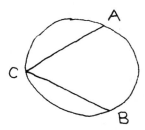

FIG. 15.4

is named in terms of the labeled points of the diagram. The sequence of named points A, C, and B naturally – as part of the organizational work of naming the angle and, from within that work, unworthy of specific comment – witnessably traces the boundary of that sector and, therein, exhibits the aperture that the angle is seen to be. The temporally placed label of an angle (Fig. 15.5) or its apparently disengaged placement in a finished figure

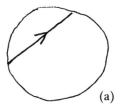
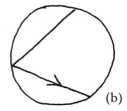
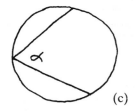

FIG. 15.5

(Fig. 15.6) exhibits this seen relationship as a proof-specific relevance. In these, and in other ways throughout the proof, the relationship between the angle and the plane sector it encloses is exhibited and, therein, maintained throughout the work of proving the theorem.

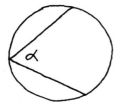

FIG. 15.6

This apparently innocuous observation – the animated character of a seen angle – is revitalized in the classification of inscribed angles that our proof used: either the center of a circle is on one of the sides or rays of an inscribed angle (Fig. 15.7(a)), it is 'interior' to that angle (Fig. 15.7(b)), or it is 'exterior' to it (Fig. 15.7(c)). That classification depends on the witnessed

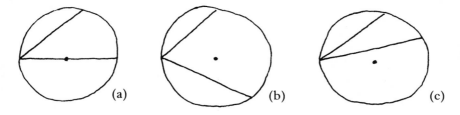

FIG. 15.7

relationship between an angle and the plane sector it bounds. The three cases are seen as being distinct and as being all the possible cases. They are practically all the cases. They are all the cases for the proof of the theorem. Parenthetically, however, it is interesting to note that the early Greeks did not have the notion of a zero angle or of an angle greater than 180°. They saw a drawn angle in terms of its smaller aperture – the more 'clearly' bounded plane sector rather than a 'surrounding' one – [this] (Fig. 15.8(a)) rather than [this] (Fig. 15.8(b)) – leaving for later mathematicians many details of proofs that, for Euclid, went unnoticed. In Euclid's time, the proof-specific relevancies of those details were simply not a part of accountable mathematical practice.

Retrospectively, the partition of inscribed angles in our proof into three distinct and exhaustive classes is seen as an *a priori*, objective, formal one, disengaged from the lived-work of its own achievement as such. What could be clearer than the fact that there are only three possible cases, that the center of a circle is either interior or exterior to an inscribed angle or is contained in one of the angle's 'sides'? In practice, as part of the work of proving our theorem, that categorization is essentially tied to the observed relationship between the center of a circle and the plane sector an inscribed angle

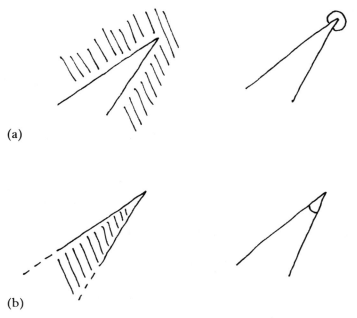

(a)

(b)

FIG. 15.8

'encloses.' But not only is the objectivity of that partition in itself an achievement of practical reasoning, the selection of such a classification is a practical accomplishment as well. It is recognized as such by a proof's production cohort. There are any number of ways in which inscribed angles can be classified, some of them relevant to other proofs of the same theorem. By first proving that the measure of an inscribed angle depends only on its intercepted arc, a proof can be given in which inscribed angles are divided into those whose intercepted arc is either less than, equal to, or greater than 180°. The relevance of such a classification is recovered from within the work of a proof; the partition of inscribed angles in our proof is the proof-specific partition that is needed to give that particular proof. The adequacy and relevance of our classification were organizational features of the lived-work of our proof, and provers expect and require this as a feature of any proof.

Even more, however, is involved in the partition of inscribed angles that was used. That partition was not just a classification, it was a temporally ordered one: the case where one of the sides of the angle contains the center of the circle was given first; then the case where the center of the circle is interior to the angle; and last, the case where the center of the circle is exterior to the angle. That order was recapitulated in the proof. It was animated as the order of cases needed to prove the theorem; therein, the original ordering was recovered as a proper one. The cases could have been ordered differently. If that different order had been followed in the proof, a more convoluted argument would have resulted. That ordering would have obscured the witnessable orderlinesses of the organizational work of the proof, thereby obscuring the proof itself. A prover would see such an ordering as an improper one and rearrange the proof so that the order of the cases, initially and in the course of the proof-account, coincided with the one that we gave. If the order of cases initially given in a proof-account is not followed later, it strikes fellow provers as obfuscating and pedagogically odd. There would be no exhibited reason for the initial ordering and, therein, it would be 'without reason.'

In a similar manner, a prover *could* temporally draw and label an inscribed angle as in Fig. 15.9. This is a crazy way of working. If a prover observes

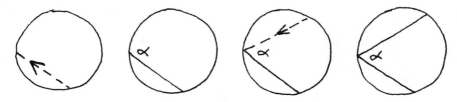

FIG. 15.9

such practices, she sees through that crazy organization of work practice to the thing – the angle – that those work practices are trying to exhibit. By finding – or, in this case, literally seeing – the intended object, the inscribed angle, the prover naturally sees – as the organizational work of producing that object – the proper way that the drawing and labeling should have been done.

Let us return to the ordering of classes of inscribed angles. From within the lived-work of our proof, that ordering has another proof-relevant, proof-specific aspect. By proving the theorem for the first case (Fig. 15.10) we then

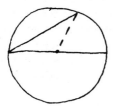

FIG. 15.10

showed that the second case (Fig. 15.11(a)) could be reduced to the first by introducing a diameter of the circle into the proof figure (Fig. 15.11(b)). The proof for the third case involved a similar reduction (Fig. 15.12(a) and (b)). The ordering of the cases is tied to the way in which the proof of the theorem reduced the proofs for the later cases to the first one.

Even when the reduction of the second case to the first is seen as a potential

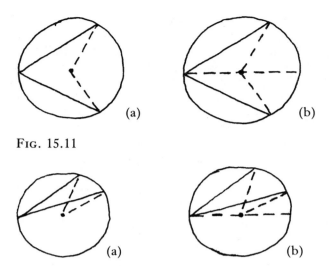

(a)   (b)

FIG. 15.11

(a)   (b)

FIG. 15.12

method for proving the theorem for the third, this last reduction is the most difficult to find. The proof for this case appeared last in our proof-account. A prover must see, in and as the material details of the proof, how that reduction is made through those details. Not only is the use of such a reduction not self-explanatory, each time the proof is re-examined the specific way the reduction is made is rediscovered as a particular and interesting method of proving. The proof-account points to that reduction, but a prover must look for and find it in the visible lines and angles of the diagram. In this, and in many other ways – in fact, essentially – our proof-account was a guide to the practical action and practical reasoning that it is seen retrospectively to summarize and describe.

A different aspect of the lived-work of our proof is illustrated in Fig. 15.13.

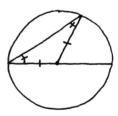

FIG. 15.13

The figure shows the markings that were used in the proof-account for the first class of inscribed angles. During that proof we discovered a proof-specific relevance of the drawn figure – that certain line segments have equal length. By exhibiting an isosceles triangle in the figure – previously hidden but then, witnessably, already there – we were able to construct the proof.

When the markings were introduced in the course of the proof, they were occasioned, expedient devices for indicating congruences, for exhibiting proof-specific relevancies of the proof-figures. They were seen and recognized as such, but also remembered as a familiar method for doing so. Although the perpendicular slash or crosshatch is seen as an occasioned, purposeful, pedagogic device, it loses that occasioned character in the presence of the objective thing – the line segments of equal length – that is seen to be already in the figure.[1] Through this lived-work, as an achievement of practical action and reasoning, the slash becomes a disengaged method for marking what the prover has disclosed through its use as an already observed and objective property of the figure that those markings simply help to clarify.

Although the congruence markers are seen retrospectively as a purely pedagogic device, the temporal order of their introduction – or the temporal order of their observed relevance in a finished proof-figure – points to a similarity between the ordering of the classes of inscribed angles and the temporal ordering of our proof-account's argument. The order in which the proof-relevant details of the figure were pointed out – first the radii, then the line segments of equal length (Fig. 15.14(a)), the fact that an observable triangle is isosceles, the implication of this for the base angles, and the witnessed marking of the particular angles of the figure described by the cited theorem (Fig. 15.14 (b) and (c)) – is a proper ordering, tied to the

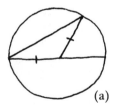 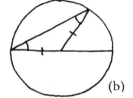 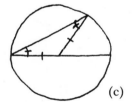

(a) (b) (c)

Fig. 15.14

organization of the lived-work of proving just this theorem. In contrast, the finished proof – as its accomplishment – has an atemporal presence. The ordering of the argument appears as an incidental feature of its exposition. The orderliness of the exposition is seen retrospectively as a proper way of exhibiting the isosceles triangle and its properties, but only as a proper exhibition – a proper description – of what was already there in the figure.

In other ways as well, the ways in which features of our proof-figures were labeled gained their relevance from within the lived, temporal course of our proof's lived-work. Minimally, we have seen that a perpendicular slash was used to distinguish and mark congruent line segments. This was never specifically articulated in the proof-account. Because the slash is used to mark segments that are analyzably of equal length – they are both radii – the slash gains the purposefulness or meaning that it has. The prover's intended purpose in using this device is itself a recognized feature of the lived-work of the proof. The notation is seen – in its intended use – to indicate found, seeable, and showably objective properties of the figure. Therein, the use of the slash appears as a completely arbitrary device. Any number of other markings, or none at all, could be used. The slash's arbitrary and incidental character is itself an accomplishment of the organizational work of the proof.

Once the slash was introduced to indicate congruent segments (Fig. 15.14 (a)), it was re-used in a witnessably analogous fashion for marking congruent angles (Fig. 15.14 (b) and (c)). More generally, the entire notation of our proof-account had a temporally developing consistency. That consistency – and, therein, the coherence of our proof-account's description of the mathematical objects involved – was consequential for the proof. Lower-case letters from the Greek alphabet were used for angles; in introducing our proof, a capital C was used to indicate and distinguish the center of a circle; *m* was used for the '*m*'easure of an angle; when points were introduced in this review to name an angle ∠ACB (Fig. 15.15), capital Roman letters were used

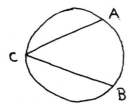

Fig. 15.15

to distinguish points from angles. Just enough notation was introduced for the proof-account that was given. And the local historicity of that developing notation, and the immediate 'context' – that is, the immediate organizational work of proving the theorem – allowed us, the local production cohort of provers, to see in a newly introduced letter, and the placement of that letter into a figure, that it was the name of the observable angle that it named. The 'α' of an angle is not seen as the 'C' of the center of the circle. The names are seen, as the cohort's situated achievement, to be the names of the things that they are (Fig. 15.16). This lived-work is an observed feature of the proof of our theorem. Yet, although it is alluded to, the description of these local notational practices is not itself a part of the proof-account nor is it found, from within the organizational work of the proof, to be a necessary thing to be added.

By rereading the proof-account of the last chapter, the reader can also see that it was filled with specifically organizational remarks indicating the first case to be treated, the end of the proof of that case, the end of the proof of the

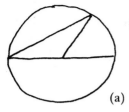 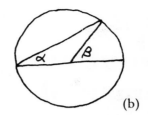

(a)   (b)

Fɪɢ. 15.16

theorem. In a sense, these are incidental to the proof; they highlight the proof's achievements. At the same time, they indicate that those achievements have been effected. There are, as well, all the 'thus's,' 'hence's, 'since's' and 'therefore's' that point to orderlinesses of work practice and to achieved descriptions of the proof's lived-work.

When a proof-account concerns a relatively simple proof whose organization and wholeness is an evident accomplishment, some of these remarks can, and often are, omitted from it. But when a proof is not elementary, they can be essential to the account, instructing a prover to examine that account and the work practices that surround it to see that everything, in fact, is there. Sometimes this same end is achieved by a written proof-account being all that there is on the page. And sometimes a proof-account is so tricky, and the organization of work practices involved in the proof so insightful and novel – a characteristic, for example, of the proof-accounts of Jean-Pierre Serre – a prover must struggle to find that organization of practice that makes the proof-account into a proof-account at all. The completeness of the proof-account – the fact that it is all that appears on the page – becomes the puzzle of that same proof-account.

Chapter 16
Built structures of mathematical practice

In the last chapter we began to see that our proof concerning inscribed angles actually had two 'parts.' The first part – what appeared in Chapter 14 and is conventionally referred to as 'the proof' – was its 'proof-account.' The second 'part' was that proof-account's own distinctive lived-work. Our proof, in fact, consisted of the 'pairing' of those two parts.

A proof-account has beginnings and endings and stages. Distinct from this, interjected into a proof-account, a proof-account formulates and describes a proof's beginnings, its endings, and its stages. A proof-account uses indexical expressions like 'since' and 'therefore,' 'hence' and 'clearly' to articulate and to claim the evidentness of the orderlinesses of the proof-account's own description and, therein, the orderlinesses of its own exhibited practical reasoning.

In contrast to this, a proof – the pairing of proof-account and lived-work – is a whole object – in fact, a social object. It has an intrinsic coherence. It has a transcendental presence – a 'massive' totality – for which 'beginnings' and 'endings' and 'stages' (or 'steps') are described features of it. In the presence of the social object – the proof – a prover can examine its proof-account to see if, practically, everything is in it and if it is a proper and practically precise description of the lived-work of the proof. A prover shapes and molds her proof-accounts so that they will be such.

In the presence of its own social object, a proof-account's designations of beginnings and endings and stages are pedagogic and, at times, artificial. A proof-account is similar to a schematicized diagram in which and through which an experienced electrical engineer sees both the constructable object and the work of its construction. In a proof, however, there is no 'distance' between the proof and its proof-account; in this way it is more like a Chinese puzzle. To solve such a puzzle one examines the way that the pieces are interconnected, twisting and turning and pointlessly pulling them, searching for the always puzzle-specific practices of seeing and turning and holding the pieces that lets them slide apart. Unlike a Chinese puzzle, a proof-account formulates and describes its own work. It is completely and hopelessly a pedagogic object – it teaches the lived-work that it itself described. A proof-account's more obvious formulations of its required organizational work – like 'first' or 'then,' 'hence' or 'QED' – articulate and describe the lived-work of the actual proof. When paired with its lived-work, a proof-account becomes the uniquely mathematical object that it is – a proof.

The beauty of Jean-Pierre Serre's work, like that of many other mathematicians, is that until a prover finds the inner coherence of his proofs – their presence as social objects – she cannot see that some of Serre's proof-accounts are proof-accounts. When she does find that coherence, she finds the new, elegant, and amazing organization of lived-work that makes up the proof. She finds as well that the proof-account Serre gave was all that needs to be said, that his proof-account is a precise description of the proof's identifying work practices and, therein, somehow, that his proof-account cannot be improved. It is the apparently unique, novel, otherwise inexpressible description of the organization of work practices of which that proof consists.

In this chapter, I continue the discussion of the lived-work of our proof that the measure of an inscribed angle is half the measure of its intercepted arc. The preceding chapter illustrated the existence of that lived-work – of practical action and practical reasoning – in a proof. The observations of this chapter are directed to illuminating the coherence of our proof's lived-work that gave our proof its observed, transcendental presence as a completed social object. Our proof concerned the objects of Euclidean geometry, and to begin, our first interest should be understanding what kind of objects these are.

Everything that was done in our proof was seen, through its circumstantial particulars, in an idealized fashion. The drawn circles of our proof-account were seen both in their idiosyncracies and for their idealized counterparts. In a sense, angles cannot be drawn, although they are. Even though they are exhibited through them, the lines of Fig. 16.1 are hardly angles. If our angles

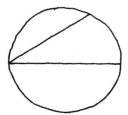

FIG. 16.1

had been depicted as infinite rays (still an obvious representation), their infinity is seen in the way that the drawing (Fig. 16.2) and the production cohort together provide for it. The arrowheads are seen for what they project as a property of an angle or for what an angle is defined to be. The centers of my circles were, at best, approximate and took up too much space to be geometric 'points.' Congruent angles and congruent radii were observably unequal, yet we visually interpreted them, seeing them *as* having the same measure.

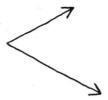

F<small>IG</small>. 16.2

None of this could have been remedied with a compass and straightedge. Although congruent angles would have looked congruent, their actual identity would have remained conjectural until it was established mathematically. The drawn radii of a circle, though they would have appeared more as congruent line segments, would have maintained their congruence not because of the precision of their construction, but because they were radii of the same circle. The objects of Euclidean geometry are idealized objects in their entirety. The work of a proof concerns these idealized objects and allows that work to be the work of proving a theorem in its intended, exhibited generality. They are the things mathematical practice produces, and a proof is a description of them.

For a local production cohort, this idealization is produced in and as the ways in which it is maintained. In any particular proof, as the developing totality – the social object – that it is coming to be, these idealizations are seen by the proof's production cohort as idealizations *in potentia*. In that our proof used only accountable properties of the various objects it concerned – like radii and centers of circles – those objects, as proof-specific ones, were realized as the proof-specific idealizations that they are. Through and as the achieved production of the whole, completed proof, the particulars of our proof became analyzable as the accountable details of proving just that theorem. Therein, over the course of our working through it, our proof itself became available as an object of the Euclidean realm. The statement of the theorem – that the measure of an inscribed angle is half the measure of its intercepted arc – became, and retrospectively is, a description of the true properties of this produced, analyzable, and objective, yet idealized, realm of Euclidean objects.

As a method of illustrating this, let us consider a curious, particularistic reading of our proof that presents pedagogic problems for instructors. A novice will sometimes see that our proof proved the theorem only for inscribed angles that look like the ones that appeared in our proof-figures. To her, Fig. 16.3 'looks' different. It is different, but not essentially so. It is not different in terms of the organization of work practices needed to prove the theorem for it.

By retracing the argument that was given in our proof-account, we see that the same argument applies to this new figure as well. First, the relevant radii are marked (Fig. 16.4). (Given its discoverable irrelevance to the proof, one

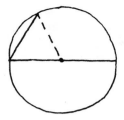

FIG. 16.3

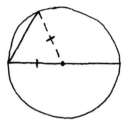

FIG. 16.4

of the figure's drawn radii is not marked, this pointing to the witnessed selectivity of the commented features of the proof-figure in the proof-account.) Again, certain of the line segments of the drawing are observed to compose an isosceles triangle and, [therefore], [its base angles] must be congruent (Fig. 16.5). The proof for this figure can proceed exactly as in the original proof.

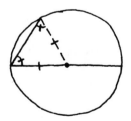

FIG. 16.5

This repetition of our proof-account's argument illustrates that our original proof, disengaged from the particular figure that appeared in the proof-account, applies equally well to the 'new' figure. Our proof supplied a witnessable and orderly method of giving the proof for any inscribed angle. The details of the proof's construction offered that construction – the proof-account – as a template of its own associated work.

A prover does not, and need not, examine other possibly different proof-figures to see that this is so. The generality of the proof-account's argument is tied to the fact that the proof-account provides for, and the prover sees, the features of the proof-figures in the idealized, objective fashion in which they are given through her own practices of proving – they are circles and radii and inscribed angles. But more particularly, over the course of a proof, as a specific relevance of the lived-work of that proof, what a prover sees is that the accountable features of the proof-figure that are used – the center of the circle, the side of the inscribed angle that contains it, the triangle that is formed – concern an entire class of inscribed angles. The proof's details neither exhibit nor suggest a more restricted domain of applicability. For any inscribed angle in the first class such as the one in Fig. 16.6, one of the sides

FIG. 16.6

or 'rays' of the angle passes through the center of the circle. That was how that class of angles was defined. Therein, when an additional radius is present as a segment of a 'ray' of a subtended central angle, the triangle that is formed will always be an isosceles triangle (Fig. 16.7).

FIG. 16.7

In this particularistic way, the generality of our proof-account's description was evinced in and as the lived, seen, material details of the proof. Our proof proved the theorem for any inscribed angle whatsoever. 'Nothing' was left out of the proof-account. The generality of our proof both is in and not in the proof-account; it is in that proof-account through the pairing of that account with its lived-work.

The locally observed and produced generality of the work of our proof is one example of how the pairing of our proof-account with its associated lived-work was maintained and examined and assessed over the temporally developing course of that proof. In order to achieve that generality, a proof-account describes the identifying detail of its own lived-work, therein making it into a proof of just the theorem it proves. The ways in which the Euclidean objects in our proof were described are identical to the ways in which their idealized character is preserved. Our proof 'lived' in the Euclidean domain because the proof-account's description and our own practical methods of working provided for that idealization and ensured that it was a proper one.

There is, however, a more subtle way in which the pairing of a proof-account with its associated lived-work is maintained throughout a proof. In a proof-account, the identifying detail of its associated proof's lived-work is rendered as a texture of description. Like a painter, the writer of a proof-account must give to that account the texture of descriptive detail that exhibits the coherence of the proof. In a manner partially analogous to an artist's drawing, the availability of the prospectively transcendental object – the proof – that is being shaped and depicted over the course of the description of its own lived-work, informs what the detail of that lived-work is that makes it the identifying detail of that specific proof. In one continuous stroke, Picasso could show us the awesome bull. For all the detail a super-realist gives to her paintings, she misses this. A proof-account is similar. The identifying orderliness of the work of a proof can be lost in too closely depicted particulars. In and as a proof, the pairing of its lived-work's produced and identifying detail with its proof-account's rendering of that detail as a texture of description is essential to the achievement of the proof as a coherent, witnessed, social object.

This texture of description is most clearly evident in our proof-account in three phenomena of the organizational work of proving. These phenomena are, in fact, endemic features of mathematical practice.

In our proof-account, we made the distinction between an angle and its measure. Rigorous definitions of both are given in the appendix to this chapter. Yet, from within the lived-work of our proof, the technicalities of those definitions were neither needed nor missed. The observable features of angles and circles and measures were sufficient for our proof. From within our proof's lived-work, nothing essential was left out for our proof to be, witnessably and analyzably, a naturally accountable proof of our theorem. Had 'all' the technicalities concerning angles and measures been introduced into the proof-account, the orderliness of the work of the proof, and therein the proof itself, would have been obscured. This balance between imprecision and technical exposition is one part of a proof-account's texture of description; in that either extreme obfuscates the actual proof, that balance is itself an organizational feature of the lived-work of proving.

A second example of this texture of description involves the fact that after observing

$$2m(\alpha) + m(\gamma) = 180°$$

and

$$m\ (\beta) + m(\gamma) = 180°,$$

our proof-account noted that, since 'things equal to the same thing are equal,' we could write

$$2m(\alpha) + m(\gamma) = m(\beta) + m(\gamma).$$

The cited reason was unnecessary. It would have been sufficient simply to claim the last equality from the preceding one.

The interesting aspect of the justification 'things equal to the same thing are equal' is its extraneousness. The basis of that extraneousness is the identifying organizational work of our proof. We all know the work practices involved in making such computations. If

$$a + b = c$$

and

$$x + y = c,$$

we can write

$$a + b = x + y.$$

We do not need the disengaged justification. We know what we want to do in the computation and the practical work involved in doing it.

As the mathematical sophistication of a prover increases, more and more proof-specific disengaged remarks such as 'things equal to the same thing are equal' are simply omitted from a proof-account. There is a tacit recognition that the practical methods of giving them are available from within the work practices of any mathematically competent fellow-prover. They cease to be relevancies for a prover's own work practices or for their proof-accounts. The practices that the justifications refer to become part of the lived, unarticulated work of proving. Their articulation distracts the prover from the produced social object – the proof. They are proof-specific irrelevancies. The work of proving a particular theorem does not occasion their introduction, nor are they necessary to see or find the produced objectivity of the proof.

Finally, let us consider a third example of the texture of description in our proof-account. Our proof used the fact that the base angles of an isosceles triangle are equal and that the sum of the angles of a triangle equal a straight angle or an angle of 180°. These theorems entered into our proof in that they were needed to describe the proof-figure – and, therein, inscribed angles – in such a way that our theorem followed as a consequence of that description. Seeing the triangle in the proof-figure as an isosceles triangle (Fig. 16.8 (a)) permitted the description of [its base angles] as being congruent angles (Fig. 16.8 (b)).

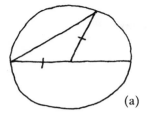
(a)

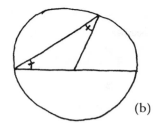
(b)

Fig. 16.8

The critical observation is that this dependence of our proof on other theorems is an exhibited feature of our proof. The fact of this dependence – the use of other theorems to describe proof-relevant details of the work of proving our theorem – was essential to our proof; the disengaged, logically-dependent structure of the propositions that were used was not. To see our proof – and, hence, the adequacy of our proof-account – we did not need to prove these other theorems first, much less the theorems they may rely on. A witnessed achievement of our proof was the *fact* of its dependence on other theorems. This balance between what is demonstrated and what is used is, again, part of the identifying detail of our proof and part of the way in which the pairing of proof-account and lived-work is maintained. But, of more immediate importance, the practical adequacy of our proof did not depend on supplying the proofs of other theorems. The practically rigorous, naturally accountable proof – our proof – was the accomplishment of our proof itself.

Underlying these lived aspects of our proof – its exhibited dependence on other theorems, the extraneous presence in the proof-account of disengaged justifications for work practices, and the proof-specific irrelevance of the 'missing' technicalities – is a produced and recognized, pervasive orderliness of the work of proving our theorem. A proof has its own texture of necessary and relevant – or identifying – detail. Its proof-account renders this texture as a texture of description. The identifying detail of the lived-work of a proof makes that lived-work into, and available as, the work of proving just the theorem it proves. It is the identifying detail of the proof as a locally produced social object. Therein, the texture of described detail is an organizational feature of the naturally accountable proof; the described lived-work of a proof-account is the (and intended as the essential) organizational work of producing and exhibiting that proof.

The lived-work of our 'simple' proof has a rich, detailed, phenomenal presence. In this and the last chapter, we began to rediscover, and to recover in its technical detail, that lived-work as an essential part of a proof – the lived-work of seeing the relevancies of a proof-figure, of finding what is being described in a proof-account, of realizing the orderlinesses of the work practices involved in a proof and in proving, of the relevance of the local historicity of things already done. We have seen, as well, the endless pointing, marking, and use of indexical expressions that fill blackboard demonstrations and mathematicians' work sessions. The presence of the prover to the proof – in fact, her embodied presence – is essential to the proof. It is an irremediable feature of a proof-account's practical, practically demonstrable adequacy.

The lived-work of a proof – the observed temporality of drawn proof-figures or the observed temporality of found features in a proof-figure, the witnessed proof-relevant details of them, the organization of blackboard or paper space and of a proof-account, the embodied presence of a proof's local production cohort, the pointing and seeing, the texture of proof-specific identifying detail, the availability of a proof's argument in its generality, the produced and discovered utility and consistency of a proof-account's notation, the pedagogic indications of beginnings and endings, of asides and steps, the 'little' practical reasoning that underlies the articulated argument and supports it – all this 'lived-work' is an essential and irremediable part of a proof. The disengaged adequacy of the proof and, therein, of its proof-account is unavailable without it.

Provers' situated work practices – the local articulation of a proof-account as a description of its own lived-work – provide unique access to the objects of mathematics. Those work practices provide for, and identically make up, the natural analyzability and natural accountability of a proof. Therein, we have begun to rediscover proofs as the vibrant, living things that they are for the local production cohorts of provers who discover and shape them in and as the work of discovering their practically rigorous proof-accounts.

What is written or said is not really the 'whole' proof. It is a proof-account. The proof – as one coherent, social object – consists of a pair: [a proof-account/the lived-work of proving to which that proof-account is essentially and irremediably tied]. The pairing – as one integral object, not as two distinct 'parts' circumstantially joined – is the 'proof' in and as the details of its own accomplishment. The uniqueness of that pairing is the uniqueness of a given proof. The multitudinous, discovered, detailed, uniquely proof-specific ways that pairing is done is the diversity and vitality of mathematical practice. The elegance and beauty of a proof depend on the way its proof-account achieves that pairing in the presence of its proof-account's lived-work. And it is through that pairing that the proof becomes the disengaged, objective, anonymous, rigorously demonstrable, analyzable, accountable object that it witnessably, from within its lived-work, is seen and discovered to be.

Appendix

From within the work practices of contemporary mathematicians, our proof had certain technical deficiencies, primarily those concerning the definitions of angles and their measure.

One way to define the notion of an angle is to define the set of angles $\mathscr{A}$ as the factor group of the even isometries $\mathscr{I}^+$ of the Euclidean plane modulo the translations $\mathscr{T}$:

$$\mathscr{A} = \mathscr{I}^+/\mathscr{T}.$$

An angle is then an element of this group, an equivalence class of even isometries. Given this definition, an angle (A, B) 'between' two rays A and B with a common vertex (Fig. 16.9) is defined as the canonical image in the

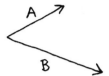

FIG. 16.9

factor group $\mathscr{A}$ of an even isometry transforming A into B. Next, a measure of angles is defined to be a continuous homomorphism ϕ,

$$\phi: \mathbb{R} \to \mathscr{A},$$

mapping the additive group of real numbers with the natural topology onto the angles with the topology given by first identifying the angles with the multiplicative group of complex numbers of modulus unity. The measure m of an angle α is then defined as the inverse image of α under ϕ:

$$m(\alpha) = \phi^{-1}(\alpha).$$

In this way, the measure of an angle is a congruence class induced under the mapping ϕ, and, thus, given a particular mapping ϕ, an angle of 30° is identified with an angle of 390° as it should be, both being, seeably, the same angle. With these definitions, the formal manipulation of the identity

$$m(\alpha + \beta) = m(\alpha) + m(\beta)$$

that we used in our proof becomes grounded in a proper mathematical theory.[1]

In our proof, the computations involving measures of angles were ancillary. We simply used the observable properties of visible angles and a convenient formalism to write them down. The technicalities involved, such as the justification that the measure of the sum of two angles is the sum of their measures,

$$m(\alpha + \beta) = m(\alpha) + m(\beta),$$

could have been avoided completely either by purposefully confusing an angle with its measure or by ignoring the distinction and relying on reasoned and analyzable properties of our proof-figures.

Using Fig. 16.10 a more 'Euclidean' proof of the first case of our theorem can be given. We wish to show that ∠ABD is half ∠ACD. Since the line segments $\overline{AC}$ and $\overline{BC}$ are both radii, △ABC is an isosceles triangle. Thus, ∠ABD and ∠CAB are equal. Since ∠ACD is an exterior angle to △ABC, it equals ∠ABD plus ∠CAB or, as we have just shown, two times ∠ABD. Therefore, ∠ABD is half ∠ACD.

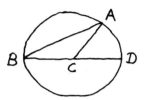

FIG. 16.10

In terms of the produced social object – the proof – the technicalities concerning the definitions of, and the distinction between, an angle and its measure are simply not missed. Now available in the sense that they are part of current mathematical practice, these 'missing' or 'hidden' technicalities were not only irrelevant to our proof but, from within its lived-work, they were not really missed at all. They were not needed for the accomplishment of the real proof of the theorem that our proof was – the accomplishment that turned our proof's practical objectivity into an achieved, disengaged objectivity. Instead, those technicalities were potential relevancies given the ways we can now examine the lived-work of our proof to find them waiting, dormantly, for their articulation as proof-account specific relevancies. From within the work of producing our proof, they may not have appeared. In fact, the work practices of proving such theorems as ours waited well over 2,000 years before those practices were given this finer accountable texture.

In addition to their irrelevance, the use of the 'fundamental' definitions of angles and measures make it virtually impossible to give a proof of our theorem. For our proof, and Euclidean proofs in general, the current, 'rigorous' definitions are only interpretively fundamental. The mathematician must be able to use them to recover all the witnessable properties of drawn angles – in other words, to be able to prove all the theorems of historical Euclidean geometry – for them to be adequate definitions. To give a proof using the 'precise' definitions, either those definitions must first be translated back into the observable details of proof-figures such as those we used or the axiomatic geometer must use a proof-account such as the one we gave, intentionally disengaged from the lived-work of its proof, to find such a sophisticated reworking of its details. In general, such renderings of proof-accounts are unreadable as proofs of the theorems whose proof-accounts they render. As we have seen many times in this *Guide*, what the fundamentalist does is reinterpret her own work and make the original proof-account an informal model of her 'essential' or 'foundational' mathematics.

Occasionally, the aim of such a sophisticated treatment is to establish the practical accountability of Euclidean proofs as a completely disengaged objectivity. Apparently, this was the aim of the first pedant, Euclid, as well. This attempt offers a curious reading of a proof-account and a misprision of its proof that purposefully ignore the proof's own witnessed achievement. The prover turns away from the phenomenon of mathematical objectivity and rigor that amazed and perplexed the Greeks as it does us today.

What this rereading actually does, and what the working mathematician wants from it, is to supply a richer accountable texture to the work practices of proving a theorem like ours. The local, organizational, lived-work of a particular proof then has a different, but not necessarily finer texture. The proof-accounts that involve their use rely on equivalently practical work methods. They are themselves practically adequate proof-accounts. By giving this finer accountable texture to their work practices, the working mathematician uses that texture to prove theorems or exhibit mathematical structures apparently inaccessible without it.

Chapter 17

The life-world structure of mathematical proofs

In the mid-1970s ethnomethodologists took up the program of studying the professions – law, physics, sociology, medicine – as sciences of practical action. For disciplines like sociology and political science, law and forensic medicine the obvious interpretation of this research program is as a claim, on behalf of practitioners, about the 'true' object of their research. For example, political scientists study the practical actions of a constituency that make up political behavior. Although not discounting this interpretation as a research proposal in its own right, the ethnomethodological recommendation is different: practitioners' situated work practices make up the heart of the professions; those *practices* are both the resource and, in the strange way that will be developed for mathematics in this chapter, the intended object of professional investigations as well. The professions are sciences of their own professional practice. Contrasting them with ethnomethodology, Garfinkel proposed that they are *classical* sciences: practitioners find the practical character of their work and reasoning – 'practical' understood in the ethnomethodological sense – essentially uninteresting, and they 'ignore' it.

This situation can be illustrated by returning to the example of a Chinese puzzle. The solution to such a puzzle is a discovery of the ways to see, hold and manipulate the puzzle so that it comes apart. The discovered solution, in fact, consists of practical action and reasoning; it is the pairing of the physical object with the practices of its manipulation in such a way that its pieces 'naturally' – as part of the course of the object's manipulation – separate. The practical actions and reasoning involved in the solution are recognized and relied on; the solution depends on and even 'describes' that practicalness. Yet, in the course of solving the puzzle, as the thing that solving the puzzle is, the pieces of its twisted metal are seen to be the puzzle and to possess all of its intricacies.

The forcefulness of claiming that the classical sciences find the practical character of their work and reasoning *essentially* uninteresting comes from the connection between that disinterest and professional *praxis*. For an experimental physicist who is not currently engaged in her work, a discovery in physics is a discovery about the physical world – about atoms and nuclei and symmetry. As part of her work in the laboratory, however, a discovery depends on the practical organization of the lived-work of experimental procedures to produce the exhibited properties of the physical object. A discovery, in fact, consists of the discovered organization of work practices that exhibits the object as well as the produced, observed, relative stability and accountability of those object-specific practices. That identity allows the object to be re-examined, reinterrogated, and its properties demonstrably exhibited once again. Yet, in their commitment to the practical adequacy of their work, physicists find the practical character of their actions and reasoning – the foundations of their science – irremediably without interest, in and as their own work as physics, as a phenomenon in and of itself. The natural accountability of a discovery – what, say, *Scientific American* celebrates and attempts to make accessible – is never, because of that natural accountability, examined as a phenomenon in its own right. A discovery is simply treated as a discovery about atoms and nuclei and symmetry.[1]

Given this circumstance, Garfinkel conjectured that 'intractable problems,' recognized by the practitioners of the classical sciences of practical action, would have to result. In discovering sciences like mathematics and physics, one such problem, and a central one, would have to be the problem of teaching discovery work, the sustaining and living heart of such disciplines. Practitioners know that if it can be taught at all, discovery work is taught indirectly under the auspices of tutorial apprenticeship. It concerns shop-work and shop-work skills. It is notoriously hard to teach, and impossible to teach explicitly.

The practical character of a discovery, and the ordinary, naturally organized work of it, are technically unavailable to practitioners in and as the work of accountably finding – and, in and as the work of finding, of accountably exhibiting – the observable, repeatable, analyzable, demonstrable discovery. This is not because they do not 'know' those skills; the skills are 'in' their fingertips. They know them, use them, rely on them; they are what they do. Those skills are the familiar, ordinary, ignored circumstances and substance of their work lives. But, in that the ways that experimental physicists work are identical to the ways that they make that work accountable, the ordinary, practical character of their work is essentially and irremediably ignored. It remains hidden in their work as that work's very accountability. What a discovery literally and identically consists of as *praxis* is inaccessible to practitioners as just that. Therein, the professions are unable to teach it.

The ethnomethodology of mathematics was the first ethnomethodological study that demonstrated, in and as mathematicians' work, that a profession is a classical science of practical action. The so-called L-pair, the topic of this chapter, provided technical access to mathematics as a classical science. It was the discovery of mathematical proofs as social objects. Rather than offering an interpretive version of mathematicians' work, it elucidated the distinctiveness of mathematics – *qua* mathematics – as a unique science of practical action. It was the discovery of mathematics as the science of provers' distinctive work practices and of provers' discoveries as discoveries about that practice.

The gentlest introduction that I know to this material is through the use of Euclidean constructions. For example, given any line segment, Fig. 17.1 shows how the perpendicular bisector of that segment can be constructed using a compass and straightedge.

FIG. 17.1

Independently of the justification of this construction,[2] the amazing thing about the figure is that, without any elaboration, just by seeing it, it shows how to construct the perpendicular bisector to any line segment. Seeing that construction is what seeing the figure is. The figure teaches the practical work and reasoning of its own construction. It is a 'pedagogic' figure through and through.

In many ways the construction-figure given above is analogous to the conversational-analytic 'first sequence,'
The baby cried. The mommy picked it up.
When the sequence is spoken, the 'mommy' is heard to be the mommy of the 'baby', and 'it' is the baby; first the baby cried, then the mommy picked it up, and the mommy picked her baby up because it was crying. By looking at the written sentences, there is nothing in the words that ensures that all these things need to be the case. The definiteness of meaning that the sequence has is both in the words and not in them. It is in the words in and as the practical actions and reasoning involved in speaking and hearing (or reading) them. That is what hearing the sequence is. Sacks's elaboration of what is heard appears not as something added to the utterances, but as a description of what hearing them consists of as practical action and practical reasoning.

The construction that the figure exhibits is, similarly, what the figure is seen to be. The seen figure is a reasoned figure, and the reasoning of the figure is what the figure is seen as. Like the conversational-analytic 'first sequence,' the figure is produced to be such an exhibition. And like the first sequence, the elaborated description of the construction is a description of things seen (heard) already to be the figure's (the utterance's) objective properties. In contrast to the first sequence, the figure shows its construction so clearly that any elaboration of it would be redundant and silly. It would lose the exactness of the construction-figure rather than clarify it. The figure itself is a precise description of the work of its own construction.

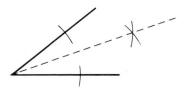

FIG. 17.2

As a second example, Fig. 17.2 illustrates the Euclidean construction of the bisector of an angle. Like the first construction, independently of its justification,[3] this figure is itself a precise description of its own lived-work. Given any drawn angle, the reader can now construct the half-line that bisects it. Not only would a verbal elaboration of the figure's construction tax the reader's patience, it would obscure the descriptive precision that the figure offers. As just one illustration, while 'the figure,' as a reasoned figure through and through, indicates a temporality of its construction – first two points on the angle's rays equidistant from the vertex of the angle are found, then a point equidistant from these – any closer description introduces a temporality that is neither a part of the figure nor an essential part of the construction.

With this preparation, an L-pair can now be introduced. The example is due to Garfinkel and concerns the proof-figure in Fig. 17.3. That proof-figure

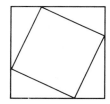 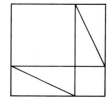

FIG. 17.3

'is' a proof of the Pythagorean theorem. On first acquaintance, what is bewildering about this figure is that it does compose a proof of the Pythagorean theorem. Once, however, that proof is seen, it takes on a transcendental, objective, accountable presence. The proof is seen as already being in the proof-figure itself. It has a substantial, 'massive' presence. It appears to have an endless depth of proof-relevant, discoverable details; these appear to be available from different perspectival viewings of *the proof's* various aspects. It withstands its repeated interrogation and is seen to be independent of all inquiries into its properties. It is seen retrospectively as the cause and source of all inquiries concerning it. It is accountably and analyzably a proof of the Pythagorean theorem.

How does this proof-figure compose a proof of the Pythagorean theorem?

As the reader will recall, the Pythagorean theorem states that the area of the square constructed over the hypotenuse of a right triangle equals the sum of the areas of the squares constructed over the other two sides. In the proof-figure in Fig. 17.3, the square on the left is dissected into four congruent right triangles and the square over their hypotenuses. The square on the right can be considered as the same square, but one in which the triangles have been repositioned to occupy the places that are shown (see Fig. 17.4). Since the total area of the square on the left and the total area of the square on the right are the same, the area of the square over the hypotenuse of the triangle must equal the sum of the areas of the squares over its two other sides.[4]

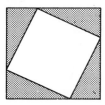 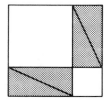

FIG. 17.4

For its local production cohort, this proof is witnessably a produced object. It witnessably gains its analyzability in and as the witnessed, lived-work of its production. All the observable properties of the proof are the achievement of the witnessed, if ignored, order-productive work of its own local production. The mathematical proof is a social object.

While the L-pair structure of proofs was the rediscovery of mathematical proofs as social objects, it was also the discovery of them as very particular and peculiar social objects. Like our proof concerning inscribed angles, the two juxtaposed figures of our proof of the Pythagorean theorem are not the 'proof.' They are a 'proof-account.' The other 'half' of the proof is that proof-account's own, distinctive, proof-specific lived-work. It is the work of seeing that proof-figure 'as' a proof of the Pythagorean theorem. The L-pair structure was the discovery that a proof consists of a pair and of a pairing: a proof is [a proof-account/the lived-work of proving to which that proof-account is essentially and irremediably tied]. When understood in terms of the lived, proof-specific, material detail of a proof, this uniquely proof-specific pairing is what any proof consists of as a social object.

If the reader examines our proof-account of the Pythagorean theorem and tries to elaborate its proof, another general feature of mathematical proofs can be seen. To argue that the total areas of the two figures in Fig. 17.3 is the same, we can observe that the length of their sides are the combined length of the two legs of the given right triangle. The property that the sum of the angles of a triangle equals a straight angle and, therefore, that the acute angles of a right triangle are acute and complementary assures us that the

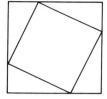 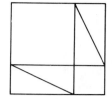

interior squares are squares. To clarify that the figures do compose a proof of the Pythagorean theorem – that the area of the square constructed over the hypotenuse of *a* right triangle is equal to the area of the squares constructed over the two sides – we must arbitrarily select one of the triangles of the figure on the left as the given right triangle and describe the interior square as the square constructed over *its* hypotenuse. Therein, as a developing aspect of the proof's exegesis, the seen, reasoned congruence of all the triangles of the proof-figure must be specifically argued as well.[5]

This elaborating argument illustrates the natural analyzability and natural accountability of the original proof-account – in this case, the proof-figure itself. We can analyze and provide elaborations of the proof-figure as a proof of the Pythagorean theorem in that the proof is already available as a social object; the accountability of our proof is a natural accountability in that it is essentially and irremediably tied to the lived, organizational work of the proof. The proof-account's analyzability is the analyzability of the lived-work of its production. An exegesis of that work is hopelessly a practical one in the presence of the achieved and observed 'wholeness' and coherence of the proof – of the pairing of the proof-account with its associated lived-work. It is hopelessly practical as well, in that it attends to the possible or imagined obscurities of the proof's proof-specific relevant detail.

The elaborating exegesis that I gave, however, sets in relief the distinguishing, uniquely mathematical character of the pair-structure of proofs. If we look at our proof-figure (Fig. 17.3) one last time, as a proof-

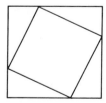 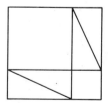

account of the Pythagorean theorem involving the rearrangement of triangles within an encompassing square, we see that, in the presence of the proof it makes available, the proof-account itself precisely describes its own lived-work. Nothing needs to be added to the proof-account. The proof-figure 'is' the proof. This is what is amazing about it and about proof-accounts in general. In the pair-structure of our proof – [the proof-account/the lived-work of proving to which that proof-account is essentially and irremediably tied] – the relationship between the two 'segments' is that the proof-account is a precise description of that account's own identifying work.

For provers, a discovered proof, or a proof rediscovered through a proof-account's mathematical examination, is the discovery of just such a pairing of account and local practice. The description that the one offers of the other becomes, witnessably, a precise description of the account's own, identifying, proof-specific lived-work. This is that pairing's unique practical accomplishment; this is what that pairing is. The L-pair is not an object in the world. It is a description of a proof that provides technical access, in and as a proof's material detail and lived-work, to that proof as a produced social object and as a situated accomplishment. The phenomenon of practical action and reasoning is not the 'pair,' but mathematical proofs – the essential and irremediable pairing of account and lived-work as a precise description of the account's own practices and reasoning.

Once a proof – the pairing of account and lived-work – is realized as a practical accomplishment, remarks that may have initially seemed to clarify its proof-account turn out, in fact, to render and distort the proof. They introduce extraneous elements into the proof; they make problematic the seen, reasoned features of the proof-account; through their argument they inject a temporality of argument into the proof-account's description that is not an intrinsic part of the proof. From within its lived-work, a proof-account – the proof-figure in our proof of the Pythagorean theorem – is everything that needs to be said or shown. The partial exegesis that I gave of our proof obscures the exhibited organization of work practices that that proof identically is.

This is, perhaps, the most interesting aspect of proofs; a proof is literally and identically a discovery about the lived-work of proving. It is a discovery of the organization of work practices of which it consists and which are described by its proof-account *as* the proof of just its theorem. Our proof-account of the Pythagorean theorem describes that organization of lived-work that makes up a proof of the Pythagorean theorem. The discovery of that proof-account, as a proof-account, was that discovered organization of practice. The amplification of a proof-account independently of its witnessed achievement – the proof – hopelessly renders that organization of work practices and distorts it. A proof-account is the discovery of the organization of proving's practices that it itself describes. In this way, through the material investigation of mathematicians' work, through the examination of particular proofs, ethnomethodologists gained technical access to mathematics as a distinctive science of the local, occasioned, situated, real-worldly, materially-specific practices of accountably proving mathematical theorems – to mathematics as a distinctive, classical science of practical action.[6]

Chapter 18

Ethnomethodological definitions, intrinsic practicality, mathematical foundations

This chapter briefly discusses three aspects of mathematicians' work. In doing so, it emphasizes some of the principal themes that animate ethnomethodological investigations. The first section indicates what it means to speak of mathematical proofs as 'naturally accountable' ones; the second discusses the practicalness of the lived-work of proving; and the third addresses the relevance of the ethnomethodology of mathematics to the classical 'foundations' problem.

Section I

Although the 'technical' terms of ethnomethodology are generally used in a manner consistent with conventional speech, their use as descriptions of practical action often makes their meaning appear strange. Ethnomethodologists investigate the problem of the production of social order through the examination of that order's material detail, not through the construction and exploitation of definitions in order to theorize about it. Definitions are themselves objects of the phenomenal domain in which the ethnomethodologist is interested. At this point in the *Guide*, however, these terms should be sufficiently familiar that a few remarks may clarify their intended use rather than obscure it. In practice, the ethnomethodologist strives to be as precise in her descriptions as possible, hoping that the descriptive character of her occasioned terminology will be evinced through the descriptive detail her writings offer.

'Accountability' is one of the central terms of ethnomethodology. The notion of 'accountability' or of something being 'accountable' (account-able) is the condition that something can be accounted for, that it is something for which accounts can be given. The ability to call an utterance a question, and the appropriateness of that naming, are part of the accountability of that utterance. 'The end of the line,' 'a place in line,' and 'the order of service' are produced and exhibited as what they accountably are. More generally, a particular organization of 'people' (a queue's production cohort) is not *interpreted* as a formatted queue, it is *seen* as one. In its idiosyncratic, queue-specific detail, it is seen as more than just a queue, but that it is a formatted queue is part of the accountability of its members' order-productive work.

The accountability of practical action is quite different from 'explanations' that are given for the organizational character of an activity. The statements that 'queues exist because we are "socialized" to stand in them' or that 'queues efficiently minimize the average time needed to allocate scarce resources' are both accounts about the nature of queues; they are predicated on the witnessed existence of queues as naturally accountable social objects – that is, as formatted queues. That someone 'butts-in-line' or 'asks a question' is itself an account of [butting-in-line] or [asking a question] – the lived-work of producing that for which the name stands as a description of that work's practical accomplishment. Minimally, the actions that 'butting-in-line' or 'asking a question' describe are seen in their particular detail, and the appropriateness of accounts of those actions is an organizational phenomenon inextricably tied to the naturally organized activity of which they are a part.

For a local production cohort, the accountability of practical action is *observably* a condition of the actions of which it is seen to consist. That an event or object is what it is, is a feature of its produced accountability as that event or object. Ethnomethodological interest focuses on the ways in which accounts are essentially and irremediably tied to the activities of which those accounts are a part, and on the ways in which a local cohort's production and management of the activities in which they are engaged are identical to the ways in which those activities are made accountable. The accountability of practical action is a phenomenon of practical action. It is investigated ethnomethodologically as an order-production phenomenon and as an achievement.

Like the notion of accountability, the ethnomethodological use of 'natural' as a description can be understood as ordinary usage. Whatever strangeness seems to reside in its ethnomethodological use results from the fact that 'natural-ness' is viewed in terms of *praxis* rather than as a disengaged state of an object or as a pre-existent state of 'nature.' The 'naturalness' of something is its practical character as an organizational feature of a naturally organized ordinary activity. It is 'natural' to [respond] to a [question] because that is what is organizationally required of it. It is 'natural' to add a column of numbers in the way that we do because that is the way we make that computation. Asking someone 'Are you in line?' is 'natural' in its connection to the problematic positioning and directed attention of the person asked, and the question is 'naturally' heard – again as a feature of the organization of the ongoing activity – as an indication of the questioner's desire to take her proper place in the queue. The accountability of these actions is an essential and irremediable part of their production as the ordinary actions that they are. Similarly, to speak of the 'natural accountability' of a mathematical proof is to refer to the accountability of that proof as it arises from within and is tied to the local circumstances and lived-work of its production, including its review and assessment. To refer to the ordinariness of mathematicians' work is not to deny the occasional, 'remark-able' distinctiveness, novelty, or elegance of it, but merely to recognize that, for provers, the lived-work of a proof is the practical, organizational work that the proof requires.

Finally, a thing's or event's 'objectivity' is viewed similarly in terms of the practices to which that word refers. Something's 'objectivity' is synonymous with its 'accountability,' 'analyzability,' 'recognizability,' 'observability,' and 'witnessability.' Consider, for example, the objectivity of a 'resonance' in sub-atomic particle physics. A discovered resonance can be regularly produced, it has demonstrable properties, and a display like the one in Fig. 18.1 is

Fig. 18.1

available to its local production cohort, i.e. experimental high-energy physicists examining the computer-generated data from an accelerator run, as the graph in Fig. 18.2, the 'bump' indicating the presence of such a resonance. Given this, if one asks what makes up a specific resonance's 'practical objectivity,' the question is identical with that of what makes up that resonance's natural analyzability and natural availability as the object which, for its local production cohort, it is.

Fig. 18.2

In general, mathematicians do not refer to the objectivity of a proof. Instead, the term 'mathematical rigor' is used. It is used, at different times, to refer both to a proof's objectivity and to its practical objectivity. In any of its uses, the rigor of a proof is seen retrospectively to reside in a proof-account, much in the same way that physicists understand the objective properties of a resonance as the properties of a 'particle' of the physical world. The natural accountability of a proof provides this retrospective illusion and allows provers to distinguish the truth of a theorem from the recognized practical character of its proof.

By exhibiting some of the lived-work of particular proofs in the preceding chapters, we began to see the presence of that work in a proof. The proofs that fill mathematics are 'naturally accountable proofs' – their objectivity or rigor is a produced feature and accomplishment of the lived-work of their production. That a proof-account is retrospectively seen to be 'a proof,' and that a prover can analyze and amplify a proof-account as a proof, is inextricably bound to the lived-work in which that proof-account has been embedded.[1] In this way, one of the consequences of the discovered pair structure of proofs is that the proofs of mathematics are recovered as witnessably social objects. This is not because some type of extraneous, non-proof-specific element like a theory of 'socialization' needs to be added to a proof, but because the natural accountability of a proof is integrally tied to its production and exhibition *as* a proof.

Section II

What does it mean to speak of the lived-work of theorem proving as consisting of practical action and practical reasoning?

Consider the following example of a Euclidean construction. Given any points P and P_1, Fig. 18.3 shows how to construct, for any n, using a compass alone, a point P_n which is n times the distance from P and P_1.

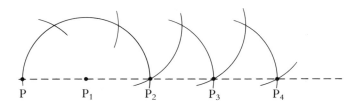

P P_1 P_2 P_3 P_4

<small>Fig. 18.3</small>

As with our previous examples, this figure precisely describes the identifying work of its own construction. A compass alone is used, and the only distance available is that between P and P_1. Thus, if it is not apparent from the figure, this reasoning indicates that the compass must be set at that distance. Since a straightedge cannot be used, the dotted line is *seen* not to be a part of the construction, but as a pedagogic aid, helping to make the figure available as the construction that was required. (A justification for the construction is given in the notes to this chapter.[2]) When the figure is paired with the lived-work that it describes, the need for such a justification is seen as a feature of the construction as well. Once that justification has been supplied – itself a proof-account – the construction-figure stands as the precise description not only of its own identifying work, but of the identifying work of the *required* construction.

This example illustrates (as have our other proofs and constructions) that once a proof or construction is seen as an intrinsically complete, witnessably produced social object, its lived-work is seen as the most practical activity in the world. The required work of exhibiting the object is so clear and so obvious – so practical – that its adequacy cannot be doubted without the doubter looking ridiculous and the material origins of the questioning being nothing if not non-apparent. If a student does not see the construction or understand its justification, what can the mathematician do but repeat what she has already said and shown? If the student asks how the mathematician knows that the same method will allow the construction of a point 100 times the distance from P and P_1, the mathematician can construct another point P_5. But if the student still cannot see the achievement of the construction as supplying a witnessably practical method, the demonstration is at an impasse.

In his *Remarks on the Foundations of Mathematics*[3], Wittgenstein gave numerous illustrations of the utterly practical character of mathematicians' work. To show that

$$2 + 2 + 2 = 4,$$

he used a diagram similar to the one in Fig. 18.4.

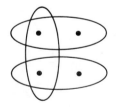

FIG. 18.4

In order to clarify Wittgenstein's argument, we can temporalize his proof as in Fig. 18.5.

•   •

•   •

4 equals 2

plus 2

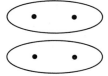

plus 2.

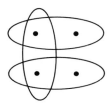

FIG. 18.5

Thus,

$$2 + 2 + 2 = 4.$$

Of course, this is all wrong; we know when to stop drawing circles around the dots. Wittgenstein's point was that, while rules for drawing only appropriate circles can be given, a prover simply 'knows' – in and as the practical exigencies of the demonstration – when to stop drawing them. Given the statement of such a rule, a prover still must recognize the practical work of its application to produce the demonstration that was originally intended.

All this is not to say that a precise description of that practical work cannot be given. What it does illustrate – and Wittgenstein's dramatic point throughout his book – is that this accomplishment is a practical one through and through. In a similar manner, when a mathematician says 'evidently' or 'obviously,' 'clearly,' 'trivially,' 'hence' or 'therefore' the word is often being used as a precise description. The work that the 'evidently' requires for a prover to see what it claims *is*, in fact, evident is so absolutely practical that, once that work is found, its evidentness cannot be doubted. The work of mathematics, for practising mathematicians, is the most practical activity in the world.

When a mathematician is engaged in serious research and is trying to prove a theorem that has never been proved before, there are no assurances that the theorem is provable or that the way she is working is adequate to find such a proof. At the same time, she is neither lost nor having proof-disengaged intuitions of the properties of mathematical objects. She is attempting to build a proof-pair. Her own local work practices, their situated character, their discovered exigencies, their occasioned character, their local, developing historicity – the practical character of her work as the work of proving – are the objects of her work and the resources she uses in it. The produced, witnessed practicality of her lived-work is the assurance that she is doing real mathematics and not 'wishing for horses.' It supports the observed, work-specific, situated character of her inquiries as being real mathematics and as exhibiting, therein, real properties of the objects she is attempting to describe. That practicality can guide her to the discovered proof (the practical character of her work is where her hopes reside), but it can also give the grounds for seeing that she is not there yet or that she is working in a manner or direction inappropriate to the discovery of the intended proof. The practicality of her work as the work of discovering a proof, and the projected practicality of her work as the work of such a proof, informs the intimate details of everything she is doing.

To this point in our discussion, the appropriateness of using 'practical' as a description of the work of proving has remained vague. To clarify that description we need to consider that the pairing of a proof-account with its lived-work makes available to provers, whether as its achievement or as a prospective one, a social object – the naturally accountable proof. From within the lived-work of proving, whether or not a proffered proof-account is a proof-account essentially depends on whether or not the naturally accountable proof – the social object – has been exhibited. It is from within the presence, or the unfolding presence, of the social object that the proof-account becomes a precise description of, and exhibits, the lived-work of a proof. The lived-work described by a proof-account is seen as the organizational work required to produce the witnessable social object. Therein, the practicality of that work resides. That practicality consists of the fact that the described work is the intrinsically (or organizationally) motivated, organizational work required to 'get the job done,' to exhibit the naturally accountable proof. It is nothing other than the work of a proof, but it is that work in and as its witnessable character as the organizational work of producing and exhibiting the naturally accountable proof that the proof-account describes.

Section III

This chapter concludes with a brief discussion of the 'foundations' problem.

Twentieth-century interest in the foundations of mathematics was stimulated by certain developments within mathematics, among them Hilbert's 'solution' of the 'invariant problem,' Zermelo's proof that any set can be well-ordered, the use of set-theoretic methods of proof, the discovery of contradictions in set theory, and, in part through Pasch's work and Hilbert's axiomatization of geometry, the discovery of flaws in the reasoning of Euclid's *Elements*. Associated with the particular difficulties involved in these developments, there was increasing recognition among mathematicians of a potentially pervasive problem. Retrospectively, a theorem can be claimed to be an obvious consequence of previously established properties of mathematical objects, but without a proof – a discovered proof-account that exhibits that proof – any such claims are conjectural. The theorems of mathematics are 'true.' They are proved true; therein, their evident truth resides. Yet, through the demonstration of the existence of potentially hidden flaws in such proofs and with suspicions concerning methods of proof themselves, the adequacy of a proof was seen to depend on circumstantial features of mathematicians' work practices.

With rare exceptions, early twentieth-century investigations of the foundations of mathematics concerned the problem of establishing the objectivity or rigor of mathematicians' work practices independently of the material details of any particular proof. Since a theorem is 'true' because it is demonstrably proved to be true, the foundations problem was interpreted as the problem of demonstrating that the lived-work of proving could be disengaged from its material-specific embodiments and be established as objective, truth-producing and truth-preserving, disengaged methods. The aim of these studies was to establish the locally produced, locally observed and observable rigor of mathematical proofs as an *a priori*, globally assured, situationally transcendent rigor; it was to turn the naturally accountable proof into a transcendentally assured, objective proof that does not depend on situated features of its proof.

There is, however, a more fundamental foundations problem. By the question of 'genetic origins' we must understand the problem of finding what, *in situ*, for a local production cohort of provers, makes their work identifiably the work of mathematics, of finding what sustains their enterprise together as the work of the discovering science 'mathematics'. The genetic origins of mathematics do not lie in the potentially problematic character of certain proofs, but in the fact that provers can demonstrate the truth of a proposition, for all provers, as their situated accomplishment. It is this daily achievement of professional mathematicians that permits and makes intelligible the attempt to demonstrate the existence of proof-independent methods of substantiating that achievement. The problem of genetic origins is, in this way, the primordial foundations problem.

The ethnomethodological discovery of the pair structure of proofs – [a proof-account/the lived-work of proving to which that account is essentially and irremediably tied] – 'solved' this foundations problem by supplying technical access to mathematical foundations as a problem for provers in the production of social order. The lived-work through which a proof-account becomes a precise description of the identifying work of a proof is identical to the work of making that proof the objective, accountable proof of a theorem. The proofs that fill mathematics are 'naturally accountable proofs' – their objectivity is a produced feature and accomplishment of the lived-work of their production. Their situated work is what makes them rigorous proofs. A discovered proof-account, as its accomplishment, *is* a precise description of its own work. That, as a witnessed accomplishment, is what the rigor of a proof literally is. The genetic origins of mathematics consist of the individual, but daily discovery and rediscovery of rigorous proofs as locally exhibited and locally produced accomplishments. It is this witnessed and recognized local achievement that sustains the prover in her discovery work. The rigorous, naturally accountable proof is what a prover's own work could projectively become because that is what she knows the practical work of proving can be.

Chapter 19
Mathematical notation and mathematical discovery

The lived-work of mathematical theorem proving has a curious dependence on its material details. On one hand, the notational particulars of a developing proof-account are essential to the discovery and description of a proof; a prover works with, arranges and examines the import and consequentiality of the 'symbols' on the page or blackboard. On the other hand, a completed proof exhibits its independence from the notational specifics of its proof-account.

This chapter brings to a close the discussion of mathematicians' work with some brief comments on mathematical notation and its essential presence in the work of mathematical discovery. In order to make the material more accessible, I have treated the proof-specific 'auxiliary' lines that are added to a proof-figure as being analogous to more traditionally conceived notational matters. The strictness of this analogy lies in the identical use of notation and auxiliary lines in and as the lived-work of proving. Rather than explicating (and exploiting) an *a priori*, principled definition of 'notation' – entertaining, for example, the discussion of 'signs' and 'symbols,' and of 'sense' and 'reference' – the examination will focus on notation as *praxis*. What are the identifying material details of a developing proof, for its local production cohort, as those details are available from with that proof's own lived-work? How is the developing material detail of a prover's work tied to the discovery of a proof?

The material presented here has less pedagogic significance than that of the preceding chapters. It describes a further aspect of the ethnomethodological investigation of mathematicians' work. However, it does concern one of the classic problems of the discovering sciences – the problem of gaining descriptive access to the lived-work of making discoveries. We have already seen that a mathematical discovery consists of a discovered organization of practical action – that is what a proof is. But how is the discovery of that organization of practical action itself a practical accomplishment?

Let us consider another proof of the Pythagorean theorem. We begin with Fig. 19.1. By introducing notation into the figure (Fig. 19.2 (a)) or more elaborately (Fig. 19.2 (b)) a computational proof of the theorem can be given. The area of the encompassing square is the area of the inner square c^2

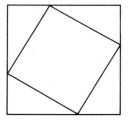

FIG. 19.1

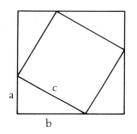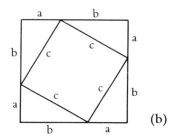

                (a)   (b)

FIG. 19.2

plus the area of the four triangles, $4[1/2(ab)]$. At the same time, the area of the square equals the square of the length of its sides:

$$(a + b)^2 = a^2 + 2ab + b^2.$$

Equating the two expressions for the area, we have

$$c^2 + 2ab = a^2 + 2ab + b^2.$$

Subtracting $2ab$ from both sides of the equation gives

$$c^2 = a^2 + b^2,$$

the area of the square constructed over the hypotenuse of a right triangle equals the sum of the areas of the squares constructed over its sides.

When a prover 'understands' the relevance of the notation for the proof ('sees' that relevance as part of the practical work of the theorem's proof), the elaboration of it in Fig. 19.2(b) is unnecessary. Already included in the notationally minimal figure is the method for the notation's 'completion' that the third figure makes explicit. The proof-account's described computation indicates the way in which the notationally minimal figure should be seen in order to make that computation and, therein, how the notation can be positioned throughout that figure (as well as how the figure should be constructed). The filling in of the proof-figure is exhibited in and as the method of the proof. When seen in terms of the practical work that the proof requires, the minimal figures give just those aspects of that work that are needed.

The other proof I want to consider is a proof that the sum of the angles of a triangle equals a straight angle. A proof-figure for that proof is given in Fig. 19.3.

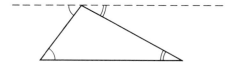

FIG. 19.3

To temporalize the figure, we begin with Fig. 19.4(a) to which a line is added parallel to the base of the triangle (Fig. 19.4(b)). Then, [this angle]

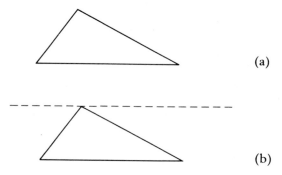

(a)

(b)

FIG. 19.4

(Fig. 19.5(a)) is congruent to [this angle] (Fig. 19.5(b)). Similarly, [this angle] (Fig. 19.6 (a)) is congruent to [this one] (Fig. 19.6(b)).

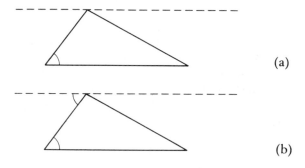

(a)

(b)

FIG. 19.5

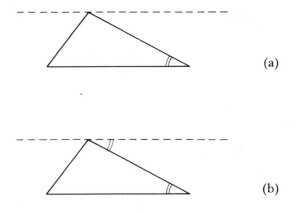

(a)

(b)

FIG. 19.6

In the full proof-figure (Fig.19.7), we see that the sum of the three angles under the introduced parallel line equal a straight angle. Therefore, the sum of the angles of the triangle equal a straight angle as well.

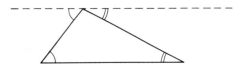

FIG. 19.7

In this example, the markings for congruent angles are themselves notational. They are used to exhibit features of the figure which, when seen, comprise the proof of the theorem. The naturally developing, naturally produced, observed consistency of these markings allows them to do this.

More important to the discovery of the proof, however, is the addition of the auxiliary line parallel to the base of the triangle. Before its introduction, the figure of an 'arbitrary' triangle (Fig. 19.4(a)) offers nothing in the way of a proof except in the manner in which a prover begins to reason about it. In order to discover a proof, the prover attempts to embed the figure within the practices of proving.[1] She looks for the ways in which those practices can supply a proof. By introducing the auxiliary line (as one possible attempt) (Fig. 19.4(b)), the relevance of that line is found in the availability of the congruent angles that the proof-figure *then*, with the auxiliary line, can be seen to exhibit. Finding the congruence of the angles that the auxiliary line makes available (Fig. 19.7), the prover therein finds the practical work that discloses the proof of the theorem – that is, she discovers the organization of lived-work that the proof identically is.

As an analogy, in an artist's charcoal sketch, the drawn lines provide the grounds for, and guide, the perceiver's eyes to see what they depict, not only the nameable object but the quality of that object – the languid nude, the awesome bull. The lines of the drawing articulate the lived-work of seeing. An artist scrutinizes a developing sketch to see whether the lines already drawn provide for the description that the sketch is in the process of becoming. The interesting thing about a drawing or painting is that it describes, not that it represents, the latter being a philosopher's conundrum.

Similar to the lines of an artist's charcoal sketch, the auxiliary lines and notation of a proof-account articulate its proof's lived-work. In proving a theorem, a prover is building a proof-account – a description of the practices of proving that theorem. The auxiliary lines of a proof-figure, the notational particulars, the proof-account as it has been developed to that point are the material details of the proof. They are not just lines and symbols; they are imbued with the practical reasoning that surrounds them – the work-specific motives for their introduction, their local historicity, their developing consistency and coherence. They are part of an unfolding description of the objects whose properties they simultaneously make available. Practical reasoning fills them, making them what they are and what their practical intention and projected use are seen to be.

Through the course of a proof-account's construction, the lines and the notation come to embody their own lived-work. The introduction of new notation, or of additional lines into a proof-figure, gives to the lived-work of a prospective proof a new and richer texture of proving's local, situated practices. The introduction of notation into Fig. 19.1 yielding (in its projected use if not its material explication) Fig. 19.2(b) makes available aspects of the proof-figure that become articulated as the practical organizational work of the discovered proof. Once again, we can compare this with the manipulation of a Chinese puzzle. From within and against the background of the lived-work of finding the puzzle's solution, the puzzle-specific manipulations through which the puzzle comes apart are discovered.

Once the completed object – the proof – is seen, the proof-account's notation becomes a proof-relevant device that is essential to the proof-account but witnessably arbitrary in its description of features of the proof's objects. The replacement of one notational schema for another is an achieved arbitrariness that the 'auxiliary' lines of a proof-figure do not have. Comparably, however, they are seen as 'auxiliary' in that they make available one and, therefore, one of any number of possible proofs of the same theorem. They take on their auxiliary character in terms of the realized, proper description the statement of the theorem offers for the achievedly idealized objects of mathematical practice.

The puzzling and amazing thing about the pair structure of a proof is that neither proof-account nor its associated lived-work stand alone, nor are they ever available in such a dissociated state. The produced social object – the proof – and all of its observed, demonstrable properties, including its transcendental presence independent of the material particulars of its proof-account, are available in and as that pairing. A prover's work is inseparable from its material detail although, as the accomplishment of a proof, that proof is seen to be separable from it. Within the building, material-, proof-, and organization-specific texture of lived-work that the developing proof-account makes available, the prover 'sees' the organization of those practices that makes up, and is, the completed proof *as* the practical organizational work of that proof. That is what 'seeing' and 'discovery' are. The discovery of that organization is the 'eureka!' of mathematical discovery.

Mathematical notation and the material detail of a developing proof-account – by producing, exhibiting, and articulating the lived-work of proving – provide a texture of description and detail of that lived-work. A prover relies on the exhibited work of notation to examine and find the proof of a proof-account. Against the background of the in-course, developing texture of situated, local work practices, a proof's organization of described work is discovered.

Mathematical discovery is frequently discussed in terms of the celebrated moments in the history of mathematics – the discovery of the binomial formula, the proof of the fundamental theorem of algebra, the discovery that the general algebraic equation is solvable by radicals if and only if its Galois group is solvable, the transcendence of pi, Gödel's incompleteness results. Not only are these discussions artificial, they present a romanticized version of mathematical genius. Herculean achievement is turned into divine inspiration; hard work is transformed into the contemplation of celestial harmony. Gauss published three proofs of the fundamental theorem of algebra before obtaining a proof of the theorem in its full generality. Prior to the publication of Gödel's paper, a number of logicians – particularly Tarski – were attempting to find a similar, self-referential argument. When Gödel discovered the method now known as Gödel numbering, he saw in its anonymity that it could be discovered by anyone and, in its practicality, that its use was 'obvious.' Had Tarski seen it yet? The abbreviatory character of Gödel's written argument, his introduction of the artificial condition of ω-consistency, the unremarked subtleties of the semantic interpretation of his constructed undecidable sentence related to the assumption of ω-consistency – in brief, his rush to publish – figure in none of the popularized accounts of his work. All of the details of his proof-account, so the story goes, are simply the evidence of genius.

The stories of genius that mathematicians propagate, and the heightened sense of discovery that popularizations give, distract attention from mathematical discovery as the ordinary circumstance and aim of provers' activities. Discovery is the condition of mathematicians' work; the genetic origins of all mathematics lie in the discovered proof. Each proof is a discovery – the elementary ones no less than the more consequential, celebrated ones. The aim of the ethnomethodology of mathematics is the examination of these vital, lived mathematical discoveries as consisting of practical action and practical reasoning.

Chapter 20

Looking back and looking forward

A considerable part of this *Guide* has been devoted to the examination of mathematicians' work. Why mathematics? Why the technical details of the lived-work of proving?

Ethnomethodologists face the same question, appropriately modified, with great regularity. Why conversation? Why formatted queues? Why a statistics exercise? Underlying that question is a more pointed one, with its implicit challenge: Why this abiding interest in the analysis of various, very particular details of ordinary, naturally organized activities? The sociologist finds nothing wrong with a sociology of mathematics, of science, of language, of 'face-to-face' interaction, of occupations, of theories of practical action and social order. Ethnomethodological studies are recognizably different. Ethnomethodologists insist on that difference. They insist on their way of conducting investigations, and they insist on their way of teaching ethnomethodology.

Superficially, sociologists' interest in the problem of social order, their intentions regarding the discovery, description, and documentation of the properties and regularities of that order, and their concern for the appropriate methods of that order's examination are similar to the ethnomethodologist's. Yet, as Garfinkel has pointed out, sociologists and ethnomethodologists differ on every issue of fact, relevance, and method; on their interpretation of every term like 'structure,' 'action,' 'theory,' 'regularity,' and 'order'; on their conception of explanation, description, detail, motive, context and justification. The two disciplines offer completely incompatible technologies for the investigation of the problem of social order.

In the early chapters of this *Guide*, I indicated some of the 'absurdities' to which sociologists' methods lead. Central to these is the fact that sociology 'misses' the natural accountability of practical action as the phenomenon of practical action and practical reasoning. The sociology and history of mathematics, for example, contain discussions of much more abstruse mathematical theorems than those examined here. They begin and end with, but leave essentially unquestioned, the natural accountability of those theorems' proofs. For ethnomethodologists, that natural accountability is the phenomenon of mathematics; it is investigated as a produced accountability. The disturbing 'mathematical-ness' of the ethnomethodological investigation is the requirement that the reader examine the technical details of mathematicians' work as those details are available to a local production cohort of provers. The ethnomethodology of mathematics itself is a peculiar pedagogy of mathematics.

In ethnomethodology, there is no requirement that everyone be interested in the intimate details of mathematical theorem proving or, as another example, in the technical way in which a co-conversationist may come to produce, at a very particular place in a conversation, a stuttering utterance. It would be ridiculous to expect this. But the idea that one could theorize the world into existence, could use disengaged methods to substantiate and justify all claims about the adequacy of one's work and the 'nature' of practical action and practical reasoning without ever examining the material details of them and without being required to do so, and could conduct studies which offer no motives from within themselves for ever needing to examine that detail is, perhaps, the greatest absurdity of traditional sociology. In sociology, every reference to the 'real world' is a reference to naturally organized settings and to practical action and practical reasoning[1]; the fundamental phenomenon of sociology is practical action and practical reasoning. Practical action and reasoning make up both the topics and resources of sociology – sociology is natural theorizing through and through. Yet, the order-productive character of practical action and reasoning is ignored. It is 'missed' not only as sociology's fundamental phenomenon, but as a phenomenon at all. And it is essentially and irremediably ignored in and as sociologists' own work practices.

In my discussion of mathematicians' work, I tried to give enough of the details of at least one ethnomethodological study to indicate some of the 'results' that it claimed and, hopefully, to give some insight into the aims and intentions that informed it. Certain technical problems, some of serious consequence for further research, were avoided; a more refined analysis would have taken us deeper into the technical details of mathematics and would have involved distinctions that gain their importance only after the material grounds and general direction of the investigation have been appreciated. The emblematic example of the pair structure of proofs is the proof-account of the Pythagorean theorem given in Fig. 20.1. Once the proof is 'seen,' the figure is 'seen' as a precise description of its own lived-work. The

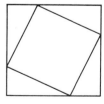
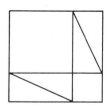

FIG. 20.1   FIG. 20.2

social object – the naturally accountable proof – is what the pairing of account and lived-work produce. But more generally, the projected availability and witnessed existence of a proof as a social object play a much greater role in the work of proving. It is proper to speak of proof-accounts only as practically precise descriptions. The witnessed precision of a proof-account is tied to the availability of the observed social object, to the way in which the settings of mathematicians' work consist of the practices of proving, and to the witnessed existence of proofs such as the ones we have examined.

The avoidance of such technical problems is advisable in a first introduction. But because these technical problems have been avoided, the ethnomethodology of mathematicians' work may have been made to seem artificially complete. The value of such an investigation resides in its consequentiality for further studies; such investigations seek to provide technical access to the phenomenon they have uncovered and, *in that way*, to the study of practical action and practical reasoning. The way in which an investigation is conducted itself consists of the practical methods that that investigation makes available, exhibits and discovers.

As we have seen with other terms of ethnomethodology, the notion of 'technical access' (and of the consequentiality of a study residing in the 'technical access' it provides) is a reinterpretation of 'results' in terms of *praxis*. The 'results' of the ethnomethodology of mathematics – like the rediscovery of the L-pair structure of proofs – are both research recommendations and findings. The practical methods that the ethnomethodological investigation of mathematicians' work uncovered give substance to the claimed pair structure of proofs as a description while, at the same time, make it available as a description. On one hand, the recognition of that pair structure affords deeper access to the practices of proving; on the other, it is part of the substance of that investigation. The L-pair structure of proofs can be exploited in further research because of the discovered methods of proving through which a proof's description as such becomes a naturally accountable one.

Criteria for the adequacy of ethnomethodological investigations appear artificial when disengaged from the investigation of the objects that they concern. The value of such investigations consists of the practical methods the investigation has uncovered, not in the fulfillment of disengaged criteria. However, from within the work of serious research, the 'unique adequacy requirement' gains its strength as one of ethnomethodology's leading research policies.

The idea of the 'unique adequacy requirement' is that, as the practical methods of an ethnomethodological investigation are themselves made available and discovered through that investigation, they increasingly make available and rediscover the methods of a local production cohort in producing and managing the naturally organized ordinary activity in which that cohort is engaged. The intention of the ethnomethodology of mathematics was for the methods of examining mathematicians' work gradually to become so tied to the practices of proving that they made available and exhibited what is uniquely identifying about those practices as the practices of real-worldly mathematics. The discovery of the practical work methods through which the ethnomethodologist gains material, technical, descriptive access to the identifying detail, for its production cohort, of a naturally organized ordinary activity is the discovery of the methods of that cohort. The 'unique adequacy requirement' is that the situated practices used (and rediscovered) by the investigator to make available and exhibit the methods through which a social object is itself produced and managed should be uniquely fitted to the local practices of which the social object consists, and must be so fitted in order to make available and exhibit the production cohort's methods.

In general, the aim of this *Guide* has been to provide an introduction to ethnomethodological research that is faithful to the work and intentions of its practitioners, yet accessible to the uninitated. It could have been organized in quite a different manner. It could have begun with ethnomethodology's central phenomenon and research recommendation:

> . . . that the activities whereby members produce and manage settings of organized everyday affairs are identical with member's procedures for making those settings 'account-able.' The 'reflexive,' or 'incarnate' character of accounting practices and accounts makes up the crux of that recommendation.[2]

The newcomer to ethnomethodology generally does not have the experience in real-worldly investigations of practical action to understand the detail and precision such statements offer. The statements become puzzles and, therein, offer themselves for theoretical reflection. Hopefully, this *Guide* has made such writings more accessible.

The heart of ethnomethodology is conducting real-worldly, materially-motivated investigations of the problem of social order. Teaching how to do this is the aim of any serious pedagogy in ethnomethodology. This book has tried to provide the background for such a pedagogy. Statements such as the one above can interest students and provide points of guidance that they can use and return to, from within their own studies, with enriched understanding. More important, under such auspices, driven by their own materially-specific interests, students can learn and discover what previously had not been even considered.

Notes

1 Beginnings

1 In an excerpt from the *Proceedings of the Purdue Symposium on Ethnomethodology* in *Ethnomethodology: Selected Readings*, ed. Roy Turner (Harmondsworth, Penguin, 1974), Garfinkel is quoted as giving the date of this study as 1945. This seems unlikely; I have given 1954 as a more probable date.

4 The problem of social order

1 The description of a Durkheimian social object follows closely the analysis given by Harold Garfinkel in his lectures. See Chapter 13.
2 From Gail Jefferson, 'Side Sequences,' in David Sudnow (ed.), *Studies in Social Interaction*, New York, The Free Press, a division of Macmillan Inc., 1972, pp. 335–6, reprinted by kind permission of the publisher. I have made minor notational changes in the transcript; the original transcript is reproduced on p. 67.

8 A statistics exercise

1 Nothing in sociology is quite what it seems. The number of publications is really an *index* of the number of publications. Only certain journals might be deemed acceptable and reviewed, relative weights would be given to these, to books, to co-authored papers, and to the order of co-authors. (In sociology the co-authors are not listed alphabetically, in part because of assessments such as those involved in tenure decisions. Like the inquiry 'What's holding up traffic?' discussed in Chapter 7, these assessment practices preserve the practical necessity of that ordering. The analyst constructing the index uses her familiarity with this practice in order to construct an appropriate index.) The index may then be normalized and approximated so as to reflect a more imaginable 'actual' number of publications. There are practical problems involved in determining the dates of tenure as well. Does the researcher understand by it the date the faculty member realized that her appointment was practically assured, the date of the faculty vote, the date of administration approval, the date of appointment? The researcher might simply send inquiries to department administrators through the department chair and use the date given to her. The selection of six years for publications reflects the fact that tenure decisions usually are made at the beginning of the sixth year. Six years accountably allows the index to reflect unpublished work that was nevertheless used as part of the faculty member's tenure appraisal.
   Most likely, the members of the faculty in the sample had widely varying careers – some enjoying sabbaticals and fellowships, others tenured after a few years of

joining the faculty. The 'data' are in every way artifactual. It is known and used as such. Moreover, the use of 'number of publications' reflects an accounting procedure that is used to justify tenure decisions, not necessarily the practices through which tenure is assessed and decided. In this light, an imaginative student might use the exercise of this chapter to document the impact of the increasing use of disengaged, 'objective' accounting practices to document and justify departmental tenure decisions to university administrators.

For an ethnomethodologist, the preceding considerations are all part of the work of producing the practically accountable and practically acceptable arguments a research paper makes. For pedagogic reasons, and as part of the local administration of course requirements, such considerations are generally relegated, at this introductory level, to a separate course on 'research methods,' except for brief comments.

2 The proper sampling procedure would have been to draw two different samples, one from those professors tenured between 1961 and 1970 and one from those tenured between 1971 and 1980. This would have legitimated the comparison between the samples and allowed the testing of various hypotheses, particularly whether the difference of means of the two samples was statistically significant. Perhaps more accurately, the error is not that each sample was not independently selected, but that the decision to divide the sample was *post hoc*. (Using two separate samples would have insured equal sample sizes and permitted an easier test, a practical consideration.) This could easily have been remedied by merely rearranging the exercise. As it stands now, the analysis performed in the exercise is an exploratory, heuristic one.

The extent to which the procedure adopted in the exercise mirrors sociologists' actual praxis is an open one. A sociologist I knew with a reputation as a methodologist once collected 'data' and constructed an index as a measure of some aspect of the population in which she was interested. A computer-generated analysis indicated that the index was not adequate for the type of analysis she wanted to do. She constructed a new index. The same problem resulted. On the third try, the new index worked. I asked her about this procedure, which seemed to me to be suspect. For each change, she was able to explain, in technical detail, the motives and appropriateness of what she had done. Another example is the friend who spent over a year 'cleaning her data' – that is, preparing the numbers available from someone else's survey for the type of analysis she wanted to do. This type of work is the *sine qua non* of statistical analysis in sociology.

Sociology's elaborate edifice of proper methodological procedures (not the practical methods that this *Guide* examines) is like a giant exoskeleton. The sociologist arranges her work practices in such a way that they can be accountably justified by reference to and manipulation of that exterior structure. The ways that she does this are, in fact, her practical methods of successfully analyzing her 'data.'

The intention of the last question of the exercise is to provide the interested student with some reflective access to the rather simplistic, ordinary, hopelessly mundane, practical reasoning that the exercise occasions.

3 The definitions of the mean, median, and mode are given as descriptive measures of the sample. In terms of probability theory, these terms are defined differently as properties of a probability distribution. The 'true' value of these measures in the population (for example, the mean number of publications of all faculty members at the selected universities tenures between 1961 and 1980) is referred to as a 'parameter.' The sample measure is a 'statistic' used to estimate the parameter.

4 These formulae and Table 8.8 were taken from Hubert M. Blalock Jr, *Social Statistics*, 2nd edition, New York, McGraw-Hill, 1972, p. 559. The original source for the table is Fisher and Yates, *Statistical Tables for Biological, Agricultural and Medical Research*, 6th edition, London, Longman, 1974.

Absolute values are taken in the formula for the test statistic because the *t*-table is given only for positive values, and this avoids further explanation.

10 The barbecue

1 M. S. Longair, *Theoretical Concepts in Physics*, Cambridge University Press, 1984, p. 1.

11 Conversational practice

1 To heighten the contrast between linguists' and ethnomethodologists' investigations, the reader should note that for linguists a 'question' is itself a technical term. It refers to the details of linguists' own work practices in examining linguistic materials, materials which are themselves prepared and cultivated so as to be adequate to those methods of analysis. In this way linguists' use of the term 'question' is fundamentally tendentious: on the one hand it trades on conventional usage; on the other it refers to technical specifications and criteria that candidate utterances must fulfill in order to be regarded as such. For the ethnomethodologist a 'question' is simply a generalized way of referring to a 'bracketed activity', a [question], for which the name 'question' is only of interest in the ways in which it is an appropriate and natural description of the activity, and of the produced achievement of that activity, that it names. Here, again, 'appropriate' and 'natural' are used to refer to the ties between a description and co-conversationists' organizational work of producing and managing a conversation's conversational events.
2 As it appears in Gail Jefferson, 'Side Sequences,' in David Sudnow (ed.), *Studies in Social Interaction*, New York, The Free Press, a division of Macmillan, Inc., 1972, pp. 335–6.
3 This may be incorporated in Jefferson's notion of 'side-sequences;' I confess to not having read the article. My aim in this and the following two chapters is to give the reader informed access to such writings, not to present an authoritative version of them.
4 See, for example, Emanuel A. Schegloff, 'Notes on a Conversational Practice: Formulating Place,' in David Sudnow (ed.), *Studies in Social Interaction*, New York, The Free Press, a division of Macmillan Inc., 1972, pp. 75–119.

12 'The baby cried'

1 R. P. Feynman, *QED: The Strange Theory of Light and Matter*, Princeton University Press, 1985.
2 An examination of this sequence appears in Harvey Sacks, 'On the Analyzability of Stories by Children,' in John J. Gumperz and Dell Hymes (eds), *Directions in Sociolinguistics: The Ethnography of Communication*, New York, Holt, Rinehart & Winston, 1972, pp. 329–45; reprinted in Roy Turner (ed.), *Ethnomethodology*, Harmondsworth, Penguin, 1974, pp. 216–32. Sacks cites a book by E. G. Pitcher and E. Prelinger, *Children Tell Stories: An Analysis of Fantasy*, International Universities Press, 1963, as the source for these utterances.

15 The lived-work of proving: first observations

1 The reader may feel that the phrase 'in the figure' here and in the subsequent text should be emended to read 'in the (Euclidean) objects that the figure depicts.' In terms of the lived-work of proving, the former phrase is, descriptively, more precise. A discussion of the idealized character of Euclidean figures is given in the next chapter. The occasions when such a figure becomes problematic as a representation of Euclidean objects 'in themselves' – and, therein, that those figures become a representational rather than a descriptive device – have their grounds in the mathematical practices involved in their use.

16 Built structures of mathematical practice

1 The interested reader may like to consult Gustave Choquet, *Geometry in a Modern Setting*, Boston, Houghton-Mifflin, 1969.

17 The life-world structure of mathematical proofs

1 For a materially motivated and fuller discussion the reader is referred to the article by Harold Garfinkel, Michael Lynch, and Eric Livingston, 'The Work of a Discovering Science Construed with Materials from the Optically Discovered Pulsar,' *Philosophy of the Social Sciences*, 11 (1981), pp. 131–58.
2 To justify this construction, the reader should note that the perpendicular bisector of a line segment is the unique line that contains all points equidistant from the segment's end points. The two points constructed in the figure are both equidistant from these end points. Since they determine a unique line, that line must be the perpendicular bisector.
3 The justification of this construction is that the triangles formed by the vertex of the given angle and the constructed points are congruent. Since corresponding angles of congruent triangles are congruent, the two angles formed by the constructed ray are equal. Hence, that ray is the bisector of the angle.
4 The suspicious reader should note that, given any right triangle, it is possible to construct the proof-figure we have used and that, since the acute angles of a right triangle are complementary, the interior squares of the constructed figures are demonstrably squares.
5 To illustrate the intricacies of elaborating a proof-account, the reader should observe that the triangles of the left-hand figure in Fig. 17.3 cannot be 'moved' within the plane of the figure to form the positioning of those on the right. While Fig. N.1 allows this, it could be seen to make problematic the fact that the figure on the right is a square. A proper mathematical exegesis of this proof ignores the seen repositioning of the triangles within the same square and introduces notation into

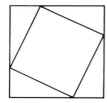 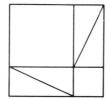

FIG. N.1

the figure so as to demonstrate the properties of the figures through it. It is another, but different, proof of the Pythagorean theorem.

6 A description of the original study of mathematicians' work is found in E. Livingston, *The Ethnomethodological Foundations of Mathematics*, London, Routledge & Kegan Paul, 1986.

18 Ethnomethodological definitions, intrinsic practicality, mathematical foundations

1 An anedote may help illustrate this situation. During the course of an advanced mathematics seminar, a particular question was referred to the resident expert, who was in fact a recognized expert in the field that the question concerned. The mathematician immediately began to 'write' with his finger on the tabletop, absorbed in the consideration of the problem. A graduate student's offer of pencil and paper was sharply declined. Toward the end of the seminar, the mathematician got up to give the solution. He wrote a single equation on the blackboard and offered it as if that equation, in and of itself, provided everything that needed to be said. He had, literally, left no traces that it could be otherwise. That equation *was* all that needed to be written; it precisely illuminated the properties of the mathematical objects involved. That, however, was the equation's accomplishment; it could be seen as the solution to the problem only through the lived-work in which it was embedded. The self-sufficient character of the written statement – in and of itself, as symbols on the blackboard – was not, and never is, available to anyone, including the mathematician that proposed it. Try as he did to obliterate any evidence to the contrary, when he was asked questions about the equation he had written, he was able to elaborate its meaning, as the naturally accountable object it was, with further comments and mathematical descriptions.

2 Figure N.2 shows that, given any two points P and P_1, it is possible to construct a point P_n *n* times the distance from P as P_1 using a compass alone.

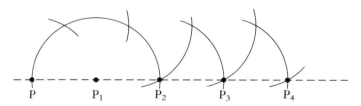

F‍ig. N.2

Although the reader will see in the figure the work of that figure's construction – and, therein, how to continue that construction any number of times – the justification of it is less obvious. The key observation is that, by using a compass whose span is the radius of a circle to plot points on that circle's circumference, that circumference is divided into exactly six equal arcs. To see this, the reader should note that the length of all three sides of the triangle in Fig. N.3 is the length of the radius of the circle and, therefore, they are equal. Since this triangle is congruent to itself no matter how it is rotated in the plan to fit onto itself, all three of the angles of the triangle must be equal, hence measuring 60°. The central angle that is one of the angles of the triangle is therefore 60°. By marking three such points on the circumference, the third point will, and must be, diametrically opposite to the starting point (see Fig. N.4).

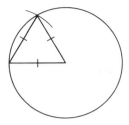

Fɪɢ. N.3

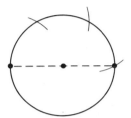

Fɪɢ. N.4

Thus, P_2 is two times the distance from P as P_1 (two times the length of the radius of the drawn circle).

In order to complete the proof, one must realize that if a semicircle is drawn with center P_2, the second constructed point on the semicircle in Fig. N.2 is the first constructed point on the new semicircle. P_3 is three times the distance from P as P, (three radii); P_4 is four times this distance, etc.

3 Ludwig Wittgenstein, *Remarks on the Foundations of Mathematics*, edited by G. H. von Wright, R. Rhees and G. E. M. Ascombe, Cambridge, Mass., MIT Press, 1967.

19 Mathematical notation and mathematical discovery

1 The natural accountability of the drawn triangle as an 'arbitrary' one already indicates the irremediable connection between the material details of a proof and the lived-work of proving. The measure of the angles of a triangle possibly could be relevant to a proof of the theorem. The proof-specific arbitrariness of the drawn figure is discovered and exhibited in the course of the proof. When first drawing a prospective proof-figure for such a proof, a prover attends to this as a prospective relevance of her work. Similarly, but observably incidental to the proof, the triangle is not positioned arbitrarily on the page but is placed so as to exhibit the parallelism of the auxiliary line.

20 Looking back and looking forward

1 See Harold Garfinkel, *Studies in Ethnomethodology*, New Jersey, Prentice-Hall, 1967, p. vii.
2 Harold Garfinkel, *Studies in Ethnomethodology*, New Jersey, Prentice-Hall, 1967, p. 1.

Index of examples